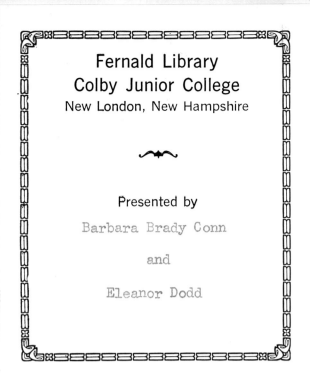

THE HERMITAGE, LENINGRAD:
BAROQUE & ROCOCO MASTERS

THE HERMITAGE, LENINGRAD:

BAROQUE & ROCOCO MASTERS

Introduction and Notes by V. F. Levinson-Lessing
and the Staff of the State Hermitage, Leningrad

ARTIA • PRAGUE
SOVETSKY KHUDOZHNIK • LENINGRAD

Edited by S. N. Vsevolozhskaya, V. K. Gerts, A. N. Izergina,
A. E. Krol, I. M. Levina, I. S. Nemilova and A. N. Nemilov

Introduction translated by A. Denešová,
Notes on the Plates translated by L. J. Lewit
Photographs by Peter Paul and Karel Neubert
Joint production of Artia, Prague
and Sovetsky Khudozhnik, Leningrad

© 1965 Artia, Prague
Printed in Czechoslovakia by Knihtisk 2, Prague
S–1912

The Hermitage collection of Italian painting of the seventeenth and eighteenth centuries is unusually rich. It admirably illustrates the work of the great masters of the Seicento and Settecento and also the regional schools. The nucleus of the collection was formed in the second half of the eighteenth and the first half of the nineteenth centuries and it was substantially expanded after the October Revolution. The collection now gives a well-rounded picture of the complex pattern of seventeenth and eighteenth-century Italian painting.

The leading personalities of the Bolognese and Roman schools of the early seventeenth century—Annibale and Lodovico Carracci, Domenichino, Guido Reni, Guercino, Albani and Lanfranco—are each represented by important works, and the only Caravaggio is one of the high points of his early period. A large canvas, *The Martyrdom of St Peter*, for a long time attributed to Caravaggio, is now given to Leonello Spada. Other artists whose work was influenced by Caravaggio are Manfredi, Preti, Gentileschi and Caracciolo. Among the foremost works of the Neapolitan school are five pictures by Salvator Rosa and ten by Luca Giordano, some of which are large decorative canvases; in addition there are pictures by Vaccaro, Gargiulio, Francesco Solimena, Conca and de Mattheis. Three fantastic landscapes with architecture, until recently attributed to the mysterious personality Monsù Desiderio (who has lately enjoyed much attention from art historians), are the work of Didier Barra and François Nomé. The Neapolitan collection is rounded out by still-lifes of Giuseppe Recco and G. B. Ruoppoli.

The Roman school of the middle and late seventeenth century is represented by Sacchi, Carlo Maratta, Pietro da Cortona, F. Lauri, P. F. Mola and G. F. Romanelli. The collection also includes outstanding pictures by the Roman eighteenth-century masters Pannini and Batoni.

Florentine seventeenth-century painters represented in the Hermitage are Cigoli, Vignali, Rosselli, Biliverti, Carlo Dolci and Furini. A large part of the Italian collection is formed by the works of the Genoese masters Assereto, Castello, Bernardo Strozzi, Vassallo, Castiglione, G. B. Carbone, G. B. Langetti, F. Rosa, Alessandro Magnasco and others. The great period of Venetian eighteenth-century painting is very fully represented in the Hermitage. Besides paintings by the foremost artists of that time—Tiepolo, Canaletto and Guardi—there are a number of works by their predecessors and pupils: S. and M. Ricci, G. B. Pittoni, Fontebasso, Carlevari, Bellotto, Marieschi and Battaglioli, and the genre painters Longhi and Maggiotto. Seventeenth-century painting is represented in the Hermitage by works of Palma il Giovane, Padovanino, Pietro della Vecchia and Liberi, as well as those of other artists like Fetti, Renieri and Loth who, though not members of the Venetian school, worked in Venice. The Northern Italian schools are also represented: Milan by del Cairo and Londonio; eighteenth-century Bologna by Giuseppe Maria Crespi; Verona by Balestra and Rotari; and Bergamo by Vittore Ghislandi.

Italian art penetrated to Russia much earlier than the art of other European countries. As early as the fifteenth-century

Italian architects had been invited to Russia, and evidence of their activity is provided to this day by the towers and churches of the Kremlin. Yet Italian artists did not stay in Russia very long, and their activity was restricted to architecture. When Russia entered into closer relations with the West in the early eighteenth century, it again turned to Italian architects. Trezzini and Michetti played an important part in the construction of St Petersburg, and the imperial gardens were decorated with statues of Venetian sculptors. A few young Russian painters went to Florence to study, and the Italian artist Tarsia worked in St Petersburg during the years 1725 and 1726. While there, he decorated the ceilings in the tsar's palace at Peterhof. Yet in spite of this artistic interchange, there were scarcely any pictures by Italian artists in the palace galleries at that time. The flow of Italian art to Russia began in the 1740s and had increased considerably in the fifties. There was a great demand for mural and ceiling paintings to decorate the newly built palaces. Small picture galleries were installed in Oranienbaum (now Lomonosov), Tsarskoe Selo (now Pushkin), and later in the Winter Palace. Noblemen built splendid residences, and their wish to decorate them with paintings initiated the first private picture collections. This heightened interest in art led to the import of pictures from Italy. The art-dealer Bodissoni twice brought large collections from Venice; the first—consisting of works by Liberi, Lazzarini, Giordano and others—went to the palace gallery in Oranienbaum, while the other was purchased in 1758 by Count Sheremetiev. The violinist of the court orchestra, Domenico dall' Oglio, also began to deal in pictures. He brought to Russia a number of canvases from Padua and Venice, among them four historical pictures by G. B. Pittoni, which later went to Gatchina Castle. Three of these (*The Death of King Candaules, Dido before the Founding of Carthage* and *The Death of Sophonisba*) have been in the Hermitage since 1925. The fourth was transferred to the State Museum of Fine Arts in Moscow in 1930. Works by Conca, Liberi and Bambini were brought to Russia by dall' Oglio and found their way into the collection of Count Razumovsky.

One of the largest private collections of that time, that of Count

M. I. Vorontsov, was formed in Italy between 1745 and 1747. In the 1740s it became quite common for Italian artists to travel to Russia for the purpose of decorating palaces and residences. They usually obtained such commissions through Italian architects and painters residing in Russia. In 1742 the Italian decorator and landscape artist Giuseppe Valeriani came to St Petersburg, followed by Ballarini, who worked there from 1753 to 1759, and later by Gradizzi, Peresinotti and Barozzi. It was Barozzi who arranged for the task of decorating the ceilings and doorways in the so-called Chinese Palace in Oranienbaum (built by Rinaldi between 1762 and 1774) to be given to the Venetian artists Zugno, Guarana, G. and A. Diziani and Cignaroli. Barozzi also arranged the purchase of forty panneaux for the Winter Palace in 1763. Rotari was one of the Italians who resided in St Petersburg from 1757 to 1762; the charming decorations depicting heads of girls, which are found in two rooms of the Chinese Palace in Oranienbaum and at the Great Palace in Peterhof, are his work. The Venetian artist Francesco Fontebasso spent two years, from 1760 to 1762, in St. Petersburg. Giovanni Battista Tiepolo, although he never went to Russia, was commissioned to paint the ceiling decorations for the Winter Palace and the palace in Oranienbaum. The list of Italian artists working in Russia at that time is completed by the painter Stefano Torelli. A native of Bologna, he taught at the Academy of Fine Arts in St Petersburg from 1762 to 1784 and executed many decorative, historical and portrait paintings.

When the newly founded Academy instituted a picture gallery in 1763, its nucleus was formed by the collection of Ivan Shuvalov, the founder and first President of this institution. Among the works bought by Catherine II from this collection for the Academy were pictures by Giordano, Celesti and Loth, as well as a set of four works by Magnasco—the *Bacchanalia* and the *Repose of the Bandits*. In 1765 forty-three pictures were moved to the Academy from Oranienbaum; among them were Giordano's *Angel appearing to King David* and two genre scenes by Maggiotto. Since 1922 this collection has been in the Hermitage, with the exception of one picture from Magnasco's *Bacchanalia* set and one of the

Maggiotto's (both of which have been in the State Museum of Fine Arts in Moscow since 1925). By the 1760s a considerable number of works by Italian, and more particularly Venetian masters of the eighteenth century were concentrated in palace and private collections in St Petersburg. Many of the more recent acquisitions of the Hermitage were originally in these collections.

In the early years of the new gallery of the Hermitage great emphasis was placed on the collection of Italian art. The Russian diplomatic representative in Venice, the Marquis Maruzzi, was charged with the task of finding and buying suitable pictures. In 1767 he took thirty-seven canvases to St Petersburg; in addition to sixteenth-century Venetian masters, these included works by Giordano, Liberi, Francesco Solimena, Ricci, Celesti, Bernardo Strozzi and a number of others. Of those thirty-seven pictures the Hermitage holds the *Tarquin and Lucretia* by Palma il Giovane, and two large pictures by Giordano, *The Triumph of Galatea* and *Rinaldo and Armida* (in Gatchina Castle until 1941). The other pictures have been missing since the first half of the nineteenth century. As the Marquis Maruzzi bought no more paintings after his first venture, it may be inferred that the majority of his purchases were mediocre.

The gallery catalogue of 1774 lists quite a few significant additions, although it has not been possible to establish how or when they were acquired. Prominent among these are two Canalettos, *The Reception of the French Ambassador at Venice* (plate 24) and *The Departure of the Doge for his Wedding Ceremony* (in the State Museum of Fine Arts in Moscow since 1930). Two landscapes with Roman ruins by Giovanni Battista Pannini, a *Virgin and Child* by Luti and the *Bacchanalia* by Cassana also entered the collection at this time. The gallery was enriched by certain works by seventeenth-century masters, Strozzi's *Tobias healing his Father* (plate 10), a work by Domenico Fetti on the same theme, and *The Concert* by Preti, at that time attributed to the French painter Valentin.

The first large collection bought for the gallery, namely the Gotzkowski Collection from Berlin, contained no Italian pictures. But the collection of Count Brühl of Dresden, acquired in 1769, included many fine seventeenth and eighteenth-century Italian paintings. Among them were works by the masters of the Bolognese academic school previously not represented in the gallery, including Reni's *The Building of Noah's Ark* (plate 6), until recently attributed to Domenichino, and Albani's *The Rape of Europa*. Since the Brühl Collection was acquired at the same time as the Dresden Gallery, the two collections had many features in common. The work of Giuseppe Maria Crespi was prominently represented in both. *The Death of St Joseph* (plate 18) and *The Holy Family*—since 1930 in the State Museum of Fine Arts in Moscow—were bought by Brühl directly from Cardinal Pietro Ottoboni, who had commissioned both works from Crespi. When Augustus III, the Elector of Saxony, commissioned Bellotto to paint a cycle of pictures portraying views of the towns of Dresden and Pirna, Count Brühl commissioned replicas for his own collection. Although these were in the Hermitage in the eighteenth century, they were taken to Gatchina before being returned to the Hermitage in 1920. Ten of them are still there, while the remaining five are now in the State Museum of Fine Arts in Moscow. One of the gems of the collection was Tiepolo's *Maecenas presenting the Liberal Arts to the Emperor Augustus* (plate 22). Other Hermitage works originally in the Brühl Collection include *The Holy Family* by Loth, *The Blessing of Jacob* by Assereto, Strozzi's *St Maurice and the Angel*, Testa's *Jacob meeting Rachel* and Cigani's *Mother Love*.

A milestone in the story of the Italian department, and indeed of the whole Hermitage, was the purchase of the Crozat Collection in 1772. Crozat had bought pictures in Italy as early as the late seventeenth century, and in 1714 he had returned to Italy to enlarge the collection of Philip, Duke of Orleans. Crozat's Collection of Italian painting included two Annibale Carraccis, the *Rest on the Flight into Egypt* (plate 3) and the *Self-Portrait*, a minor work by Ludovico Carracci, *The Holy Family*, an important Reni, *The Youth of the Virgin Mary*—originally the property of Cardinal Masarini—and an excellent study, also by Reni, *The Repentance of St Peter*, from the collection of the Cardinal Savelli in Rome. Crozat also owned a fine Guercino, *The Vision of St Clare* (plate 7) and four works by Domenico Fetti, including the *Portrait of an Actor* (plate 9) from the Masarini Collection, as well as the *David* (now in the State Museum of Fine Arts in Moscow, but once the property of Charles I, who acquired it with the whole collection of the Duke of Mantua). The Roman school was represented in the Crozat Collection by Sacchi's *Hagar in the Desert* and *Divine Wisdom*, Carlo Maratta's *Adoration of the Shepherds* and *The Annunciation*, as well as Romanelli's *Hercules and Omphale*, and two works by P. F. Mola, *Jacob and Rachel* and *Rest on the Flight into Egypt*.

In 1779 the Hermitage acquired the equally important Walpole Collection. In it the Bolognese school was represented by a number of altarpieces. There was an early Carracci, *Lamentation over the Dead Christ*, Reni's *Dispute of the Church Fathers on the Immaculate Conception* and Albani's *Baptism of Christ*. Nearly all the works by Salvator Rosa in the Hermitage descend from the Walpole Collection, including the *Portrait of a Man* (plate 12), *The Prodigal Son*, *Democritus and Protagoras*, and *Odysseus and Nausicaa*. There were two monumental works by Luca Giordano, *The Forge of Vulcan* (plate 13) and *The Dream of the Young Bacchus*, and Maratta's *Portrait of Pope Clement IX* (plate 11), as well as two signed works by the Genoese master Vassallo, which were originally attributed to Castiglione.

The Baudouin Collection, acquired in 1781 in Paris, was much poorer in Italian works than the Crozat and Walpole collections; moreover, most of its Italian paintings were of secondary importance, with the exception of the *Portrait of a Poet*, attributed to Francesco del Cairo, and the *Self-Portrait* by Giuseppe Maria Crespi.

In addition to the big collections, the gallery bought single pictures in the 1770s and 1780s. Among the more important pictures acquired in this way are *Evening Landscape with Fishermen* by Annibale Carracci, *Cleopatra* and *The Rape of Europa* by Guido Reni, Guercino's *St Jerome*, *The Betrothal of St Catherine* by J. Vignali, *St Cecilia* by Carlo Dolci, *St Sebastian* by Balestra, and works by Sassoferrato, Maratta and a number of others.

In addition to these acquisitions, the gallery also bought works by contemporary Italian artists. Whereas in the 1760s the interest of Russian art-buyers had been focused mainly on Venice—where decorative pictures were purchased to hang in the palaces and homes of the aristocracy—attention in the 1770s was diverted to Rome and the new classicist school there, which was led by Batoni.

In 1767 Ivan Shuvalov went from Paris to Italy, remaining there until 1773. Keenly interested in the art of ancient Rome, he collected antique sculpture and pottery, and he established close relations with the artists of Rome. Shuvalov negotiated a commission for two history paintings with Batoni— *Thetis entrusting Chiron with the Education of Achilles* (Batoni was engaged in painting a cycle of pictures on the story of Achilles at that time) and its companion *The Continence of Scipio*. Both works date from 1771 and were housed in Gatchina Castle during the nineteenth century, from where they were returned to the Hermitage in 1926. Another Batoni, *The Holy Family*, came to the gallery in 1789. It had been painted for the Grand Duke Paul Petrovich during his travel through Europe in 1787 and had been presented by him to the Empress Catherine. At the close of the eighteenth century the gallery had a wide selection of Italian seventeenth and eighteenth-century pictures. However, one important artist not represented in the collection was Caravaggio; and the Hermitage did not succeed in filling this gap until the beginning of the nineteenth century. The Napoleonic wars and the revolutionary events in Italy brought the large private collections of several Italian noblemen into the market. Among them was the Giustiniani Collection in Rome, founded in the late seventeenth century. The collection, brought by a dealer to Paris, was on view in 1812 and was purchased for the Berlin Museum three years later. Some of the pictures, however, had been sold previously; in 1808 F. Labensky, the keeper of the Hermitage Gallery, had bought Caravaggio's *Lute Player* (plate 1) and *The Martyrdom of St Peter*, which was until recently also attributed to Caravaggio, but is now thought to be the work of his pupil L. Spada. The second of these pictures must have attracted a great deal of attention in Russia, since the secretary of the Academy of Fine Arts, V. I. Grigorovich, wrote a special article about it in the *Journal of Fine Art* in 1823. Yet Russian art-lovers were still interested primarily in the seventeenth-century painting of Bologna and Florence; so much so, that until halfway through the nineteenth century the Hermitage enlarged its Italian department almost exclusively with works of these two schools. In 1808 Labensky also bought L. Carracci's *Christ carrying the Cross* and a small picture by Guercino, *Apparition of the Virgin to St Lawrence*. An interesting work by the Sicilian painter Novelli was acquired in the belief that it was by a seventeenth-century Bolognese master. When the collection of the Empress Josephine was acquired in 1814, the Hermitage gained two typical works of the seventeenth-century Florentine school, Carlo Dolci's *St Catherine* (plate 8) and *Tobias and the Angel* by Biliverti. Also acquired at this time were two pictures by Cagnacci and Cantarini, both pupils of Guido Reni. In 1819 Prince Trubetskoy, who had been requested to buy pictures for the Hermitage on his travels to France and Italy, purchased Annibale Carracci's *Christ appearing to the Holy Women*—since 1930 in the State Museum of Fine Arts in Moscow—and Carlo Dolci's *Mary Magdalen*. Another Dolci, *St Anthony*, was acquired together with other pictures from the Duchesse de Saint Leu in 1829. A magnificent Annibale Carracci, *The Three Marys at the Tomb* (plate 5) and Cozza's *Joel*, at that time attributed to Domenichino, were bought in 1836 from the banker Coesvelt in Amsterdam. In 1843 Guercino's *Assumption of the Virgin Mary* was brought to St Petersburg from the Tanari Palace in Bologna, and in 1850 Labensky's successor, Fedor Bruni, obtained Guercino's *Martyrdom of St Catherine* and Reni's *St Joseph with the Christ Child* in the sale of the collection of William II, King of the Netherlands.

From this list of acquisitions a consistent trend becomes apparent. The gallery was interested chiefly in the most important seventeenth-century masters; moreover, in accordance with then prevalent aesthetics, almost exclusively in the Bolognese academic school. Works by other artists entered the Hermitage only occasionally; for example, in 1826 two landscapes by Zuccarelli were purchased in St Petersburg, and in 1829 the gallery acquired Marieschi's *The Rialto Bridge in Venice*, believed to be a Canaletto. Easily the most significant work acquired abroad was *Lamentation over the Dead Christ* by Luca Giordano, which was purchased in Paris in 1810. Several interesting Italian paintings bought for the Hermitage were thought to be works by Spanish artists who were not very well known in Russia at that time. From the Coesvelt Collection came two canvases regarded as Ribalta's—*The Martyrdom of St Catherine* by an unknown early seventeenth-century Italian master, and *Joachim and Anna*, the only work in the Hermitage by the Neapolitan master Massimo Stanzione. An arresting Venetian eighteenth-century painting, *An Old Man Reading*, was purchased in St Petersburg in 1817 in the belief it was painted by Velasquez, and shortly before that *Ephraim's Sacrifice* by the Venetian Pietro della Vecchia had been purchased with an attribution to Ribalta.

During the latter half of the nineteenth century the collection of Italian Baroque painting remained almost unchanged. S. A. Gedeonov, the director of the Hermitage Museum from 1863 to 1877, was interested mainly in the great Renaissance masters and in antique art. His successor, Prince Vasilchikov, turned his attention to the pictures in the palaces and palace storerooms, trying to improve those departments of the gallery that had been neglected, especially the collection of eighteenth-century art. In 1882 Tiepolo's splendid work *Maecenas presenting the Liberal Arts to the Emperor Augustus* was transferred to the Hermitage from Gatchina Castle; four years later the first Francesco Guardi, *View of a Town*, was purchased from the Golitsyn gallery in Moscow, and another Guardi, *View of a Square with Palace*, was acquired in St Petersburg in 1895. One of the pictures bought in 1897 from the Prince Lobanov-Rostovsky Collection was *Diana and Endymion* by Pittoni. A valuable work by Domenichino, *St John the Evangelist*, rounded out the extensive collection of Bolognese painting. Tsar Nicholas I acquired it from D. A. Naryshkin, whose collection dated from the early nineteenth century and in 1881 it was given to the Hermitage.

The first serious attempt to make a through investigation of the Italian collection was by E. Brüningk, who prepared a catalogue of Italian and Spanish works for publication in 1889. After Brüningk's untimely death Ernest von Liphart, for many years keeper of the gallery, published a newly compiled and detailed catalogue of the Italian and Spanish departments in 1912. Liphart also studied the pictures in the various palaces, above all in Gatchina Castle, and in private collections in St Petersburg, discussing them in a series of articles in the journal *Starye Gody*.

After 1900 the collection of Italian seventeenth- and eighteenth-century painting remained generally unchanged, except for a few individual works donated to the gallery. In 1912 Count P. Stroganov bequeathed a fresco by Domenichino, *St Andrew*, to the Hermitage; and on the request of Liphart, Prince S. M. Volkonsky, donated a large early Tiepolo, *The Rape of the Sabine Women*—at that time attributed to Ricci.

In the years following the October Revolution many important pictures came to the different sections of the Hermitage and the Italian department made significant acquisitions. Alexandre Benois, then director of the gallery, deserves credit for the efforts he made to reorganize the Italian collection to give a more complete idea of the realistic streams in Italian painting, and a better representation of the Genoese, Neapolitan, and above all the Venetian schools.

As early as 1922 it was possible to hold an exhibition of newly acquired Italian paintings in three large rooms of the Winter Palace. Although few paintings were acquired in the following decade, individual pictures have been bought occasionally since 1936.

During the twentieth century the least number of additions have been made to the collection of painting of the Bolognese school, as this had been given much care in the past. In 1923 Albani's large-size canvas *Landscape with Three Marys at Christ's Tomb* came to the gallery from the collection of Countess S. V. Panina. From Gatchina Castle came two sketches by Lanfranco for oil paintings commissioned to decorate the church of San Paolo fuori le Mura, in Rome, *The Spies with the Grapes from Canaan* and *The Widow of Zarephath*. A sketch by Guido Reni, *Bishop Andrea Corsini*, was transferred from the Stroganov Palace in 1922, and Guercino's *Sybil* entered the gallery in 1938. Of greater importance was the entrance of a number of works by the Carravaggists. Among them the *Bacchus*, by a painter whose identity has not yet been

established (although Liphart himself attributed the picture to Caravaggio, so close is it to his style), deserves attention. It was purchased in 1919 from a private collection. Other works by Caravaggists that came to the Hermitage after the Revolution were Manfredi's *Lute Player* (from the Shuvalov Collection in 1925); *The Vision of St Clare*, an interesting work by a master close to Caravaggio (perhaps M. Preti), which was transferred in 1923 from Gatchina Castle where it hung as a Caravaggio; and two pictures by Renieri, *St Sebastian* and *St John the Baptist*, acquired from private collectors during the years 1923 and 1924. In 1937 the gallery bought an arresting work by Gentileschi, *Samson and Delilah*. The Neapolitan school was enriched by no fewer than seven Giordanos, the most important of which, *The Battle of the Centaurs and the Lapiths*, came from the Stroganov Collection. The 1958 catalogue attributes this work erroneously to Pietro da Cortona. Equally significant were four large paintings of biblical scenes by the same master, *The Angel appearing to King David* (from the Museum of the Academy of Fine Arts, St. Petersburg), *The Birth of John the Baptist* and *Christ driving the Money-changers from the Temple* (both from Gatchina Castle), and *The Sacrifice of Isaac* (from a private collection). In 1921 a magnificent Solimena, *Rebecca at the Well* (plate 14), was discovered in the Great Palace at Peterhof, and it was transferred to the Hermitage, which had previously had only pictures of secondary importance by Solimena. The inventive Gargiulo achieved his rightful place in the gallery only with the purchase of *The Adoration of the Golden Calf* in 1923—from the Myatlev Collection, founded in the late eighteenth century. In 1931 the Neapolitan school was enlarged by the arrival of Conca's large canvas, *Solomon's Idolatry;* the latest addition has been a work by Conca's pupil Francesco da Mura, which came to the Hermitage in 1948 from the collection of the great writer A. Tolstoy. The Genoese school was enriched by some valuable additions, notably Strozzi's large *Allegory of Fine Arts*, from the Stroganov Palace. From the Palace in Pushkin came *Satyrs bringing Presents*, a characteristic work by Castiglione, who had not been represented until then in the Hermitage. Another gallery acquisition was the cycle of seven Magnascos from the Academy of Fine Arts, which we have already described, and two splendid Magnasco landscapes (plates 15 and 17) acquired in 1919 from the well-known collector Prince V. Argutinsky-Dolgoruky. Other important additions were Langetti's *Samson*, Francesco Rosa's *Daedalus and Icarus*—both were transferred from Gatchina Castle in 1923—and two pictures by Valerio Castello.

Two landscapes by Locatelli, who was previously not represented in the Hermitage, enlarged the collection of works by the Roman school, together with several Batonis, two of which were returned from Gatchina and two transferred from the Academy of Fine Arts (*Religion—the Patroness of Science and the Arts* and *Beauty lured by Wealth*), and *Hercules at the Crossroads* from the Yusupov Collection. The only Panninis in the Hermitage had been views of Roman ruins, now the gallery obtained two church interiors by Pannini, again from the Yusupov Collection. In 1920 the gallery acquired a landscape by Vanvitelli, *View of Rome*, from Gatchina Castle.

New acquisitions also improved the collection of seventeenth-century Florentine painting. Vignali's *Abraham and Three Angels* was acquired from the Yusupov Collection, two works by Francesco Furini (who had not been represented before) were added, Rosselli's *David's Victory* was purchased in 1939 and in 1947 the Hermitage bought Dolci's *Martyrdom of St Andrew*. The number of pictures by North Italian masters has increased substantially. In 1923 the gallery obtained Francesco del Cairo's imposing work *The Death of St Petronilla* which is now attributed to Pignoni; and from the Yusupov Collection came Francesco Londoni's *Peasant Family*. Six works by Giuseppe Maria Crespi were added; Crespi is the outstanding figure of the eighteenth-century Bolognese school. Two of the new Crespis acquired by the Hermitage were *The Laundress* (plate 20) and its companion, *Woman searching for Fleas*, both purchased in 1939. Italian portraiture, entirely absent from the Hermitage until 1917, is now at least partly represented by *Portrait of Countess A. A. Chernishev* by Stephano Torelli, *Portrait of a Boy* (plate 21) by Vittore Ghislandi, *Portrait of Prince A. B. Kurakin* by Batoni and *Portrait*

of an Abbot by Rotari—all these obtained between 1921 and 1923. Three genre pictures by Todeschini, one of the most interesting exponents of North Italian realism, were also acquired. Another gap in the Hermitage's Italian collection was filled when several good still-lifes were acquired.

The most exciting additions to the Venetian school were five large Tiepolos on themes from Roman history. Painted for the Venetian patrician Dionisio Dolfin, they were brought to Russia in 1886 from the Miller von Aichholz Collection in Vienna; the remaining three pictures of the series are now in the Metropolitan Museum in New York. The magnificent *Landscape* by Francesco Guardi (plate 27) was discovered by the custodian of Gatchina Castle, V. K. Makarov, in the neighbourhood of Gatchina, and handed over to the Hermitage in 1928. At about the same time the collection gained two Canalettos, three Marco Riccis, and three paintings by Carlevaris. Until then there had not been any works by the two last artists in the gallery. Two works by Sebastian Ricci were acquired from the Yusupov Collection in 1925—*The Childhood of Romulus and Remus* and *Abraham and the Three Angels*. A third picture by Ricci, *Venus and Cupid*, was purchased in Leningrad in 1949.

Although the Hermitage's collection of Italian seventeenth and eighteenth-century painting is undoubtedly rich, it still has regrettable gaps. C. Saraceni, A. Caroselli, B. Cavallino, G. B. Piazzetta and Bombelli are not represented at all. We hope that it will be possible to acquire works by some of these artists in the future.

The collection of Spanish painting in the Hermitage was second only to the collection in Spain itself until the beginning of this century. Even now, at a time when leading European and American galleries are bidding for the great Spanish masters to complete their collections, the Hermitage can well compete with the other major collections. The excellence of its Spanish department is demonstrated by the great number of Spanish artists represented here, including many outstanding works of the greatest masters.

The place of honour in the collection must go to the twelve

Murillos. Of the three works by Ribera, two date from the master's early period. The *St Lawrence* by Francisco de Zurbarán (plate 41), who is represented by two more canvases, ranks among his finest works. Less justice is done to the work of Velasquez, however; besides the early genre picture *The Breakfast* (plate 36) there is the *Portrait of Count Olivares* (plate 39), very expressive yet insufficient to demonstrate the great masters achievement. El Greco's *St Peter and St Paul* (plate 28) is the only work of the master in the gallery, but it is a particularly great one. In addition to the giants of Spanish painting there is a wide selection of works by excellent artists, such as Antolinez, Valdes Léal, Cano del Mayno, Pedro Orrente, Pareja, Pereda, Antonio Puga, Francisco Ribalta, and several other less important artists. Apart from these, the Hermitage has a very good collection of Spanish sixteenth-century art; besides the El Greco, there are pictures by Pantoja de la Cruz, Coello and Morales. The only major gap in the Spanish collection is the absence of any work by Goya.

Because Spanish painting was little known during the seventeenth and eighteenth centuries in the rest of Europe, there were few Spanish pictures in galleries and private collections. The only exception were the palaces and castles of the Hapsburgs, whose dynastic ties permitted them to obtain a number of outstanding Spanish portraits. The best known of the Spanish masters were José Ribera, who worked in Naples, and Murillo, whose work gained great popularity about the middle of the eighteenth century. The gentle charm of the women and children in Murillo's pictures and his delicate palette were in perfect harmony with the taste of the time. Murillo was the first Spanish painter to have his work hung in the Hermitage. In 1768 Diderot arranged for the purchase of Murillo's exquisite *Rest on the Flight into Egypt* (plate 47), which was available when the collection of Gaignat, the former secretary of Louis XV, came up for sale. This painting had been acclaimed by Parisian art-lovers, because of its affinity with religious pictures by van Dyck. A second Murillo on the same theme came to the Hermitage in 1772 with the Crozat Collection. In the same year Murillo's *Boy with a Dog*

(plate 45) and its companion, the *Girl with Fruit and Flowers*—also known as *The Orange Seller* (since 1930 in the State Museum in Moscow)—were acquired from the Paris sale of the Duc de Choiseul's Collection. The purchase of the Walpole Collection in 1779 brought three more works by Murillo, including the large *Immaculate Conception*. Finally, in 1792 the Hermitage obtained a fine replica of the well-known *St John the Baptist with a Lamb* from the collection of Prince Gregory Potemkin, the original of which is in the National Gallery, London.

It was about the same time that the first works by Ribera and Velasquez appeared in the gallery. In 1769 Ribera's *St Jerome in the Desert*, dated 1650, came from the Brühl Collection; a little later *St Onuphrius* was added. How the Hermitage came to possess one of the most fascinating works of Velasquez's early period, *The Breakfast* (plate 36), is still uncertain; in the gallery inventories of the eighteenth and nineteenth centuries it is listed as the work of an unknown Flemish master. It was forgotten entirely until 1895, when it was identified as a Velasquez and installed in its proper place. The Spanish campaign of the Napoleonic wars in the early nineteenth century greatly affected the fate of many art treasures in churches, monasteries and palaces. A number of pictures were included in contributions imposed by Napoleon's generals and sometimes made part of the war booty. The property of noblemen suspected of sympathizing with Napoleon was confiscated and sold by the Spanish Government, and as several monasteries were also closed down a considerable number of pictures came on the market. French and English art-dealers promptly travelled to Spain. Lebrun assembled a large collection in 1807 and 1808; when it came up for auction in Paris two years later, most of it was sold to England. At the same time the leading English art-dealer, Buchanan, sent the artist Wallis to Spain as his agent. In his arresting memoirs, published in 1824, Buchanan tells what happened on that expedition. Wallis's great ingenuity in concluding agreements, both with French generals and with neutral diplomats, enabled him to circumvent government orders that no Spanish pictures should be removed from the country. When Wallis ran out of money in Madrid, he approached W. G. Coesvelt, the Amsterdam agent of the British banking house of Thomas Hope & Co. Acting on Wallis's advice, Coesvelt assembled an excellent collection of Spanish masters which he shipped to Amsterdam. From this collection Alexander I acquired in 1815 sixty-seven Spanish masterpieces for the Hermitage.

The Coesvelt Collection, from which the Hermitage also enriched its Italian department, was one of the great collections assembled by English financiers at the beginning of the nineteenth century. Unlike the relatively stable art collections of the British aristocracy, most of which remained more or less intact until the close of the nineteenth century, the collections of financiers and businessmen were generally sold during their owner's lifetime to the leading European art galleries and museums. In this way the collection of John Angerstein, purchased in 1824 by the British Government, formed the basis of the British National Gallery; the Solly Collection was bought in 1823 by Friedrich Wilhelm III for the Berlin Museum; and the larger part of the Coesvelt Collection went to the Hermitage.

Among the major works that came to the Hermitage with the Coesvelt Collection were Velasquez's *Portrait of Count Olivares* (plate 39) and *Portrait of Philip IV*, an excellent version of the 1655 portrait in the Prado. *The Laughing Boy*, a work of de Villavicencio, was also attributed to Velasquez. From the Coesvelt Collection came the Hermitage's first Zurbarán, *The Virgin Mary as a Child* (plate 42), del Mayno, *The Adoration of the Shepherds* (plate 32), two still-lifes by Pereda (plate 49), Puga's *Knife Grinder* (plate 40) and Ribalta's *The Raising of the Cross* (plate 31), as well as two other works attributed to Ribalta—*Mary Magdalen and Apostles at Christ's Tomb* and *Portrait of Lope de Vega*. The works by Murillo in the Coesvelt Collection were *The Annunciation* and *St Joseph with the Christ Child*, and there were several works by lesser artists, including Iriarte, Carducho, Coello, Tobar and Mathias de Torres.

In 1808 Wallis obtained three Murillos from the collection of the Marquis Santiago in Madrid, among them a large canvas, one of the series of pictures on the life of Jacob, the son of Isaac, executed for the Marquis de Villamanrique, the Pro-

tector of the Academy in Seville. The remaining pictures of the cycle became part of the contribution paid by the City of Madrid to General Sebastiani. Two of them, *Jacob's Ladder* and *Isaac blessing Jacob* (plate 43), were obtained for the Hermitage in 1811, while the remainder of them went to England in 1814 with most of the other works from the Sebastiani Collection. *Jacob's Ladder* and *Isaac blessing Jacob* rank among the finest Murillos in the Hermitage. In 1852 the collection of Maréchal Soult came up for auction in Paris. Bruni, the keeper of the Hermitage Gallery, managed to buy Murillo's *Liberation of St Peter*, which was destined originally for the Madrid hospital La Caridad, as well as Zurbarán's *St Lawrence* (plate 41). A further Murillo, *The Vision of St Anthony*, purchased in 1852 from a Parisian art-dealer, had been taken out of Spain by one of Napoleon's generals. The Hermitage had also acquired some valuable Spanish works with the collection of the Duchesse de Saint Leu in 1829; among them was Ribera's *St Sebastian and St Irene* (plate 34). The Spanish revolution of 1820 again turned the eyes of Europe towards Spain. More Spanish private collections changed hands. In 1831 the large collection amassed by the minister of Charles IV, Don Manuel Godoy, Principe de la Paz, was auctioned in Paris. In that auction the Hermitage obtained Murillo's *Death of the Inquisitor Pedro Arbuez* (until 1804 in the Church of the Holy Inquisition in Seville), the large *Three Saints in Prison* (then attributed to Ribalta but now believed to be the work of R. Rizi), and an early Ribera, *The Vision of St Jerome*. In 1834 the Hermitage bought fifty-one paintings from the Spanish Ambassador in Petersburg, Paez de la Cadeña. Although his collection as a whole was not outstanding, it brought to the gallery works by artists who had not been represented before, including Antolinez, Valdes Léal and Collantes. During the previous year the Russian Consul-General in Cádiz, A. Gesler, had offered to procure pictures from Spain for the tsar. He attached a list to his letter, suggesting, among others, four pictures by Velasquez. Although the keeper of the gallery, Labensky, protested that most of the works listed were of secondary importance, the collection was purchased. It was found that Labensky had been absolutely correct; not only were the majority of the pictures in poor condition, but none of the presumed Velasquez canvases was genuine. The only work that might have been of any value to the Hermitage, the *Equestrian Portrait of the Infante Charles II* by Carreño de Miranda (influenced by the well-known Velasquez *Portrait of the Infante Don Balthazar*), was thought to be unworthy of the gallery and sent to Tsarskoe Selo, only returning to the Hermitage in 1886. Without waiting to hear from St Petersburg, Gesler sent another eleven pictures, which were supposed to include works by Goya. These, however, were returned to him and his offer of further acquisitions for the Hermitage was declined. At this time Baron Taylor bought some pictures in Spain on the order of Louis Philippe for the king's famous 'Spanish Museum' in the Louvre. After the revolution of 1848 this large private collection was returned to its previous owner and put up for auction in 1853. Most of the paintings from the collection are now in leading European museums, although unfortunately the Hermitage failed to acquire any of them. In 1845 the former Russian Ambassador to Spain, D. P. Tatishchev, bequeathed his collection to the Hermitage. Although the collection contained few Spanish works there were some arresting pictures, including the *Portrait of the Commander of the Order of Santiago de Compostela* by Juan Pareja, the assistant and pupil of Velasquez, and an excellent example of the work of the mannerist Morales, *The Virgin with Child*.

In 1850 the Hermitage attempted to acquire some full-length portraits by Velasquez. Bruni went to the Netherlands for the sale of the collection of the Dutch king, William II, and succeeded in obtaining some valuable Netherlandish and Italian works. But, the portraits which he had acquired as the work of Velasquez were later found to be no more than competent studio copies. Of these, Mazo's *Portrait of Philip IV* still has to substitute for Velasquez's full-length portraits; the *Portrait of Count Olivares* was transferred to the State Museum of Fine Arts in Moscow in 1930. The 1852 acquisition of works from the collection of Maréchal Soult completed the gallery's Spanish department, which hardly changed until 1917. The only exception was a single, very fine El Greco, *St Peter and St Paul*. The work was in the collection of G. P. Durnovo, and was first shown in public on the occasion of an exhibition of masterpieces from private collections held by the journal *Starye Gody* in 1908. The owner, in whose family the El Greco was since the mid-nineteenth century, donated the work to the Hermitage in 1912. It is not known how the work came to Russia.

Since few works by Spanish masters were in private hands in Russia, few came to the Hermitage after the October Revolution. Several works by Spanish masters from the Khanenko Collection found their way into the Museum of Western and Eastern Art in Kiev; those in the Shuvalov Collection were acquired by the State Museum of Fine Arts in Moscow.

The gallery's acquisition in the early post-revolutionary years included Zurbarán's large *Crucifixion* (previously in the Marble Palace)—this is a version of a theme dear to the master's heart—*The Guardian Angel* by Juan del Castillo, which was transferred from Gatchina in 1926, and a signed Antolinez, *The Annunciation*, which arrived from Ropshinsky Palace two years later.

The Hermitage's collection of French paintings, especially from the seventeenth and eighteenth centuries, is generally considered to be second only to that of the Louvre. The close ties between Russia and France and the interest of Russian collectors in French art made it possible to build an outstanding collection in which all the great French masters—Poussin, Claude Lorrain, Le Nain, Watteau, Chardin and Fragonard and many others—are well represented. The Hermitage also has a fine collection of French drawings, sculpture and applied art. The one exception, however, is the absence of any work by de la Tour.

French art made the first appearance in Russia in the second half of the seventeenth century, when three Russian ambassadors, sent to the court of Louis XIV, brought to Moscow among other royal presents magnificent tapestries. But closer artistic ties were established only during the visit of Peter the Great to Paris in 1717.

At that time a new trend, typified by Watteau's *L'Embarquement pour l'Ile de Cythère*, began to make itself felt in French art.

But Peter and his entourage, preferring the *grand art* of Louis XIV, made extensive inquiries about the centres of tapestry weaving in France, as well as about the medallions which celebrated the life and reign of *le Roi Soleil*. A series of Jouvenet tapestries on themes from the New Testament was presented to Peter and is still in the Hermitage. The *Tenture des Indes* served as the model for the first tapestries manufactured in the newly founded St Petersburg works. During his stay in Paris, Peter the Great had been painted both by Rigaud and Largillière and again by young Oudry. Unhappily, none of the portraits has been preserved, and only engraving of the work by Rigaud and preparatory drawings for the Oudry portrait exist. At the tsar's request the artist Jean Marc Nattier went to the Hague to paint a portrait of Catherine I and on his return to Paris painted a companion picture of Peter in full armour. Both works were in the Winter Palace until 1918, when they were transferred to the Hermitage.

A group of artists had been called to Russia to assist in an ambitious scheme of town-planning, including the construction of the palaces in the neighbourhood of St Petersburg. Among the group were the architect Alexandre Leblond, the sculptor Bartolomeo Rastrelli and the master of decorative carving Nicolas Pineau, as well as a number of draughtsmen, engravers, cabinet makers and gardeners. But Nattier (who had painted a scene of the Battle of Poltava for Peter while at The Hague) and Oudry refused their invitations, so that Peter was forced to choose a lesser artist, Louis Caravaque of Marseilles, as court painter. Caravaque, who stayed on in Russia for the rest of his life, painted many portraits of Peter and Catherine I, although the Empress Elizabeth was more often his subject. He also executed a few of historical scenes, and his *Battle of Poltava* (where Peter the Great defeated Charles XII of Sweden in 1709) is now in the department of Russian Cultural History in the Hermitage. A later arrival at the tsar's court was François Jouvenet, the younger brother of Jean Jouvenet. The portrait on horseback of Peter, which he executed in Paris in 1719, is now in the depository at Pavlovsk Palace.

There was not a single work by a French painter in Peter the Great's Collection; commissions to French painters and purchases of French pictures were to come later. The only exceptions are the two battle-scenes (one of them, *The Battle of Lesna*, is in the Hermitage) which the tsar commissioned from Denis Martin the Younger, a pupil of Louis XIV's famous court painter of battle pictures, A. F. van der Meulen.

During the reign of Elizabeth interest in French art increased considerably. From 1756 to 1758 Louis Tocqué worked as a court portrait painter in St Petersburg. The Hermitage has some of his works, among them a full length portrait of the Empress Elizabeth.

When in 1757, on the initiative of Shuvalov, the St Petersburg Academy of Fine Arts was founded, its organization and teaching system were based on that of the Royal Academy of Painting and Sculpture in Paris. The architect Vallin de la Motte, the sculptor Nicolas Gillet and the painters Louis Le Lorrain, Lagrenée the Elder and Jean Louis de Velly were invited to join the staff from France, and the engravers Radigues, Bonnet and Henriquez came later. De Velly stayed in Russia until 1780, and was particularly successful with portraits. The Hermitage has his *Self-Portrait* (transferred in 1920 from Gatchina Castle) which shows the artist in his studio, at work on a portrait of I. I. Shuvalov. Langrenée stayed in St Petersburg for only two years (1760–1762), during which time he painted pictures for the Academy, the Empress and private clients. His *A Roman Woman's Love for her Father* came to the Hermitage from the Museum of the Academy in 1922, while other paintings by Lagrenée are in the Russian Museum and in the Tretyakov Gallery.

The greatest French artist working in St Petersburg during this time was Etienne Maurice Falconet, who remained in Russia twelve years and created the famous monument to Peter the Great. The painter J. B. Le Prince lived in St Petersburg from 1758 to 1763, executing paintings on ceilings and over doors in the Winter Palace. He travelled extensively while in Russia, even making a journey to Siberia, and brought back a wealth of drawings on which he later based paintings, cartoons and engravings. His picture *The Russian Baptism* earned him membership of the Paris Academy in 1765.

Less well-known French artists active in St Petersburg in the latter half of the eighteenth century included the portrait painter Jean Louis Voille (who lived there between 1770 and 1793), the old painter of historical scenes Gabriel Doyen and the portrait painter Jean Laurent Mosnier. Both Doyen and Mosnier emigrated to Russia during the first years of the French Revolution and died in St Petersburg. Another artist from France was the famous Elisabeth Louise Vigée-Lebrun who spent six years in Russia, and painted many portraits during her stay there.

In the 1750s I. I. Shuvalov and I. G. Chernyshev began to acquire French works for their collections. A. S. Stroganov bought a number of pictures during his stay in Paris from 1770 to 1779. A little later the Yusupov Collection was formed—this was particularly rich in French art—and finally, at the turn of the century, Chancellor A. A. Bezborodko amassed his large collection. The Shuvalov and Stroganov collections much later enriched the Hermitage, as did partly the Bezborodko Collection. The Gotzkowski Collection, which was the first collection acquired for the gallery in 1763, had few French works, among them Bon Boulogne's *Marriage of Hippomenes and Atalanta* and Courtin's *Vestal Virgin*. Soon the flow of French art to Russia increased. In 1766 Catherine II was advised by Diderot to authorize Prince Dmitry Golitsyn to obtain Greuze's *The Paralytic*, a work that had captured Diderot's fancy. Catherine even considered inviting Greuze to St Petersburg, but when Diderot warned her of the artist's unpleasant character the plan was abandoned. In 1782 Melchior Grimm made an unsuccessful attempt to buy Greuze's well-known work *L'Accordée de Village* (now in the Louvre). In 1766 Prince Golitsyn approached Chardin with a commission for a picture on *The Attributes of Art* (Plate 79) for the St Petersburg Academy of Fine Arts. The painting was brought from France by Falconet and was placed in the Hermitage gallery until 1854, when the picture was sold by auction. One of the picture's later owners used it as an overdoor picture in his country seat near St Petersburg. When it was discovered in 1918 in a St Petersburg antique shop, it was returned to the Hermitage. Another work Falconet brought to Russia was a large Boucher, *Pygmalion and Galatea*,

which was destined to decorate the ceiling in the St Petersburg Academy of Art (now in the Hermitage).

Two years later Prince Golitsyn was again authorized to commission one picture each from Boucher, Joseph Vernet, Louis Michel Vanloo the Younger, and Vien. Yet Diderot protested that Boucher was irresponsible and unreliable and Vernet too busy, so their commissions were withdrawn and given instead to de Machy and to the Italian artist F. Casanova, who was living in Paris. Diderot insisted that Vien's *Mars and Venus* represented an allegory of peace. Yet when the picture arrived in St Petersburg it was received badly, being sharply critized by Falconet. It was transferred from the Hermitage to Gatchina and was only returned to the Hermitage in 1925. Falconet found equally sharp words for Louis Michel Vanloo's *Sextet* (*The Spanish Concert*), yet was delighted with *The Triumph of Galatea* by the artist's father, Jean Baptiste Vanloo, which had been acquired in the sale of the Gaignat Collection in 1768. Shortly before that date eight sketches for paintings in the chapel of St Gregory in the Dôme des Invalides had been purchased from the third member of the Vanloo family, Carle. Only one of these is still in the Hermitage.

Since Catherine II was not particularly interested in contemporary French painting, few French pictures were brought to Russia in the 1770s and 1780s, but the work of Carle Vanloo appears to have been very popular in Russia. Catherine kept up a correspondence with Mme Geoffrin, whose salon was popular in French literary and art circles at the time. In 1772 Mme Geoffrin offered Catherine two pictures, *The Concert* and *La Lecture*, which she had commissioned from Carle Vanloo, for only 1,200 francs. The Empress paid Mme Geoffrin 30,000 livres for these same two paintings. Melchior Grimm commented on this transaction in his *Correspondence Littéraire*: 'To buy pictures to sell again is an excellent investment.' In 1772 Vanloo's *Self-Portrait* was acquired, while *The Sultana drinking Coffee* and *The Sultana with Embroidery* were purchased ten years later from the St Petersburg art-dealer Clostermann. Although Catherine had another Vanloo, *The Sacrifice to Cupid*, nothing is known of the fate of that work.

The purchase of pictures from Parisian collections began in

1766, when one of Poussin's finest works, *Tancred and Erminia* (plate 54), was acquired in the sale of the collection of the artist Aved. In 1769 Diderot tried unsuccessfully to obtain the collection of French masterpieces of La Live de Jully, which was sold in Paris the following year. In that auction the Hermitage acquired, among others, a pair of large canvases by J. F. de Troy—*Lot and his Daughters* and *Susanna and the Elders*—dating from 1721.

A substantial enrichment of the still limited Hermitage French collection came with the acquisition of the Brühl Collection of Dresden. In the Brühl Collection were Poussin's *Deposition from the Cross* and two Watteaus—*The Embarrassing Proposal* (plate 67) and *Rest on the Flight into Egypt*—which had come from the collection of Jean de Julienne. In 1771 the collection of Councillor François Tronchin was bought in Geneva. Tronchin was an art connoisseur and friend of Diderot, Vernet and Prince Golitsyn. We have no exact information about the works he owned, as the catalogue Tronchin compiled and published in 1767 has not survived. We do know, however, that Tronchin had two landscapes by Claude Lorrain (*Evening in the Harbour* and *The Road to Emmaus*) both of which are now in the Hermitage, and the *Woman Bathing* and *Jupiter and Io* by F. Lemoine. In the following year the Crozat Collection was sold in Paris. Secured in its entirety for the Hermitage, it was as rich in French masterpieces as it was in the treasures of Italian, Flemish and Dutch paintings which so greatly enriched the St Petersburg gallery. Crozat housed his collection in a special palace whose interior had been decorated by La Fosse, Oppenord and Watteau. He had some four hundred paintings, nineteen thousand drawings and a large collection of cut gems and other art treasures. After Crozat's death in 1743 his drawings, engravings and gems were sold; the gems were bought first by Philip, Duke of Orleans, and then acquired in 1782 by Catherine II, before making their way to the Hermitage. The paintings from the Crozat Collection went to his nephew, the Marquis du Châtel. After the Marquis's death in 1750 the collection was split between his two brothers—President Tugny and Baron de Thiers. When the Tugny pictures came up for sale in 1751, Thiers bought the best of them, thus becoming the owner

of a huge art collection which he continued to enlarge. Yet immediately after his death in 1770 his heirs began to negotiate the sale of his art treasures. Diderot invited Tronchin to act as an expert, and negotiated with them for ten months before he chose three hundred and forty-two pictures. The sale of the Thiers Collection to Russia caused a great deal of adverse publicity in France, and the director of the Royal Collections, Marigny, complained bitterly that he did not have sufficient funds to keep the collection in France. While the negotiations were still going on, Diderot wrote to Falconet: 'The wrath of all society has turned on me; and do you know why? Because of the pictures I am sending you. Collectors are complaining, and so are artists and rich men. What incenses and humiliates them most is the fact that the Empress is going to acquire the Thiers Collection while her country is at war.' Diderot was referring to the Turco-Russian war of 1768–1774. French art-lovers protested most vehemently at the sale of works by Raphael, Reni, Van Dyck, Rembrandt and Poussin. Although the Poussins in the collection (*Cupids and Genii*, *Cupids on the Hunt* and *Satyrs and Nymphs*) do not show him at his best, it contained pictures by almost all the important French seventeenth- and eighteenth-century masters, from Valentin and Vouet to Watteau and Chardin. Notable works were Valentin's large *Christ driving the Money-changers from the Temple*; Vouet's *Virgin and Child* and *Venus and Adonis*; a big canvas by Lesueur, *Darius Opening the Tomb of Nitocris*, three pictures by Bourdon, among them the superb *Death of Dido* (plate 63); La Hyre's *Mercury entrusting the Infant Bacchus to the Nymphs* (plate 62), Le Nain's *A Visit to Grandmother* (plate 52) and *Italian Landscape* by Claude Lorrain. The Crozat Collection also contained works by N. Loir, P. A. Patel, J. Stella, J. F. Millet and Le Bourguignon. Prominent among the eighteenth-century masters was Watteau, who was represented in the Crozat Collection by *Actors of the Italian Comedy* (also known as *Return from the Ball*), *The Hardships of War*, and *Respite in Wartime* (all of these are still in the Hermitage, but *The Bivouac* was transferred in 1928 to the State Museum of Fine Arts in Moscow). Other important works of French painting obtained with the Crozat Collection were Chardin's *Washerwoman* (plate 76), a sketch by Largillière for the painting *Preparations for the Gala Banquet held at the Paris City Hall, 30th January, 1687* (plate 65), Charles de la Fosse's *Hagar in the Desert*, Lancret's *Concert in the Park*, a large sketch by P. Subleyras, *Portrait of a Woman* by F. de Troy, and *Young Woman with a Veil* by J. B. Santerre.

The French collection of the Hermitage was soon enlarged when Diderot acquired two excellent landscapes by Poussin—*Landscape with Polyphemus* (plate 57) and *Hercules and Cacus in a Landscape* (the latter has been in the State Museum of Fine Arts in Moscow since 1930)—from the Marquis de Conflans, who had lost his property at cards. The Hermitage catalogue of 1774 lists some more additions to the French section, whose provenance has not yet been established. Among them were four Lancrets, notably the splendid *Portrait of the Dancer Camargo* (plate 70), Greuze's *Portrait of a Young* Man, *Rest on the Flight into Egypt* and *Pastorale* by Boucher, Chardin's *Grace before a Meal* (*Le Bénédicité*) (plate 78), and a splendid still-life by Oudry. Further acquisitions of those years were two battle-pieces dating from Poussin's early period (one of them was transferred to the State Museum of Fine Arts in Moscow in 1930), Poussin's *Esther before Ahasuerus*, Lorrain's *Odysseus approaching the Court of Lycomedes*, E. Lesueur's *Presentation of the Virgin Mary*, and many less important French seventeenth- and eighteenth-century works.

The next big event was the acquisition of the Walpole Collection in 1778. With it the Hermitage gained *Moses striking the Rock* (plate 56) and *The Holy Family* by Poussin; *Morning in the Harbour* (plate 59) and *The Bay of Baiae* by Claude Lorrain; as well as *The Massacre of the Innocents* by Bourdon and *The Finding of Moses* by E. Lesueur. Although the purchase of the Baudouin Collection in Paris in 1781 enriched the Dutch collection, it brought only a few French pictures to the Hermitage, notably Vernet's *Storm*. Vernet's work, which was so popular with Russian collectors of the time (Stroganov, Yusupov, Bezborodko and others), did not find a place in the Hermitage until the early nineteenth century, although Paul I became interested in the works of Vernet and Greuze. Already in 1782, when he travelled about Europe under the name of the Comte du Nord, he commissioned several pictures

from Vernet. Another artist enjoying great popularity at that time was Hubert Robert; almost every Russian collector had one or more of his pictures of landscapes with architecture. Stroganov set the trend by buying five pictures from Robert in 1773. Then, in order to get Catherine interested as well, he commissioned from Robert a painting of the *Ruins in Tsarskoe Selo* to be painted from drawings sent to him. The finished work arrived in St Petersburg in 1791. No pictures by Robert hung in the gallery, but Tsar Paul ordered four large decorative compositions from the artist for his palace in Pavlovsk, as well as several other pictures.

The most interesting of all the works purchased singly for the Hermitage between 1774 and 1789 are Watteau's *Savoyard* (plate 66) and Louis Le Nain's masterpiece *The Milkmaid's Family* (plate 50). Another of the pictures acquired from the St Petersburg art-dealer Clostermann was Lancret's *Spring and Summer*. In 1781 the Hermitage obtained the splendid *Portrait of a Boy with a Book* by Perronneau from the collection of A. G. Tieplov. Since Perronneau was in St Petersburg at about that time, it is possible that Tieplov bought the picture direct from the artist. In 1792 Catherine acquired for the Hermitage the collection of Prince G. A. Potemkin, and the French department gained a large Mignard, *The Magnanimity of Alexander the Great*. During the short reign of Paul I only one French picture was bought, but it was Fragonard's excellent *The Farmer's Children*.

At the beginning of the nineteenth century the character of the gallery's acquisitions changed entirely. Attention was now focused on the work of Vernet and some of his contemporaries, including M. Gérard, J. L. De Marne, N. A. Taunay and L. M. Bilcoque. The majority of pictures were bought in St Petersburg, but funds were made available to Vivant Denon, the director of the Napoleon Museum, to buy pictures, and Labensky went to Paris in 1808 for the same purpose. Among the pictures he brought back with him was one work by a French seventeenth-century master, Philippe de Champaigne's *The Prophet Moses* (acquired at the auction of the well-known Choiseul-Praslin Collection). When the entire collection of the Empress Josephine at Malmaison was purchased in 1814, the

Hermitage was fortunate to acquire the superb series of paintings by Claude Lorrain, *Morning*, *Noon* (plate 61), *Evening* and *Night*. In 1822 the Hermitage had bought Mignard's *Portrait of J. B. Colbert*—then attributed to de Champaigne—in the St Petersburg sale of the Korsakov Collection.

No major changes took place in the French Hermitage collection during the next fifty years, although some pictures were taken to palace storerooms, while others were sold by auction in 1854. In 1882 the Hermitage's director, A. A. Vasilchikov, drew attention to the many works of art that should be brought to the Hermitage from the various crown properties and palaces, and some pictures were transferred to the Hermitage from Gatchina, notably Boucher's *Landscape with a Pond* (plate 73) and *The Messengers of Geoffrey de Bouillon with Armida* by F. Lemoine, as well as two small battle-scenes by J. B. Pater. In 1898 pictures by A. F. van der Meulen were transferred to the Hermitage from Tsarskoe Selo, and from Peterhof came one Grimou in 1905 and one de la Fosse in 1907. An outstanding acquisition was Fragonard's *The Stolen Kiss* (plate 82) which came from the collection of King Stanislav Augustus at Lazienki Palace in Warsaw. Greuze's *Head of a Girl* was purchased from A. I. Somov, the gallery's keeper, in 1890, and among the works bought by the Hermitage in 1897 from the collection of Prince A. J. Lobanov-Rostovsky was Sebastian Bourdon's *Portrait of a Man*.

At that time both the great halls housing French painting in the Hermitage were so overcrowded that there was no place to hang further additions. After the Revolution when the Winter Palace became part of the museum it was possible to extend the collections with works from Imperial and several private collections. In 1922 an exhibition of newly acquired French painting from the seventeenth and eighteenth centuries, which was larger than the entire pre-1917 collection, was held in the new gallery in the former Winter Palace. Only a part of the works then shown, however, remained in the Hermitage; the rest was handed over to the State Museum of Fine Arts in Moscow—together with many other paintings from the Hermitage.

One of the works shown at the 1922 exhibition, Poussin's *Holy Family with St Catherine and St John the Baptist*, which originally belonged to Silvio, Cardinal Valenti-Gonzaga, in Rome, and passed later into the possession of Stroganov before entering the Hermitage. Together with four other Poussins, previously in the Hermitage, it went to the State Museum of Fine Arts in Moscow in 1927. From the Stroganov Collection came two more important works by Poussin, the *Rest on the Flight into Egypt* (painted for Chantelou in 1657–8 and mentioned in Poussin's letters) and the *Bacchanal*, an example of Poussin's production in the 'thirties). In 1931 an unfinished Poussin, the *Rescue of Queen Zenobia*, was found among the anonymous pictures in the depositories of the Museum of the Academy of Fine Arts. Several preparatory sketches for the work were already known. Another important work was Claude Lorrain's *Landscape with Dancers*, which came to the Hermitage in 1930 from the Stroganov Palace.

From Gatchina came two pictures in 1925 which the Hermitage catalogue of 1958 still attributes to Vouet. Charles Sterling has since established that one of them was the work of the eminent seventeenth-century painter Jacques Blanchard. *Hercules among the Olympians* (from the Brühl Collection) is considered by Sterling to be the work of Vouet's pupil François Perrier. Neither Blanchard nor Perrier had been represented in the Hermitage before. A characteristic example of Vouet's work, the allegorical figure *Minerva*, came to the gallery in 1931.

From the Yusupov Collection came a large Laurent de la Hyre, *St Germain blessing St Genevieve*, of 1630. In 1946 the Hermitage obtained from a private collection in Leningrad an early signed Stella, *Lucius Albinus giving up his Coach to the Vestal Virgins*, which is dated 1621. The fine collection of French seventeenth-century landscape paintings was further enriched by several good examples of the work of Etienne Allegrain, previously unrepresented in the gallery, as well as pictures by J. Lemaire, Dughet and Millet.

A group of excellent French seventeenth-century portraits came to the Hermitage in 1923 from the family seat of the Myatlev family. Alexandre Benois had first catalogued their collection in 1906; it contained Jean Daret's *Self-Portrait* (plate 53).

H. Gascard's *Portrait of the Journalist de la Fond*, Vivien's *Portrait of the Architect Jules Hardouin Mansard*, and the *Portrait of an Unknown Man* by Jean Jouvenet. From the Olive Collection, the Hermitage acquired the valuable *Portrait of Hortense Mancini*, at the time thought to be by Mignard, but in actual fact the work of the Flemish painter Jacob Ferdinand Voet who worked in Paris and Rome. The work of Voet, which has only recently been subjected to detailed study, is represented in the Hermitage by two more paintings.

Some pictures were discovered in the palaces; these included a signed Pierre Montallier, the *Seven Acts of Mercy*, found in Peterhof, an interesting example of French realism from the latter half of the seventeenth century. Also from the Peterhof came Jouvenet's *Deposition from the Cross* and two works by de la Fosse. Several of the Watteaus in the Hermitage went to the State Museum of Fine Arts in Moscow; but the two which came to the Hermitage—*The Holy Family* from Gatchina Castle and *The Capricious Girl* (plate 69) from the Stroganov Collection, were examples of the master's late period. Both these pictures had come from the Walpole Collection. Also in the 1922 exhibition were three decorative paintings from the Marble Palace, attributed to Watteau, both by Benois and V. Miller, but now given to his school. Almost certainly the work of Watteau, however, is a superlatively fine landscape which had been until 1931 in the museum at Kaluga. In 1933 the Hermitage's collection of paintings from the school of Watteau was enriched by a work of J. B. Pater, *Women Bathing*, from Peterhof, and in 1920 by four pictures by N. Lancret, among them the arresting *Marriage Contract*.

Five new Bouchers came to the Hermitage after the Revolution from the Olive Collection, the most significant of them being *Landscape near Beauvais* (plate 71). The Amsterdam Museum recently acquired a finished preparatory drawing for the painting. Mention, too, should be made of the *Virgin and Child* by Boucher's teacher F. Lemoine (from the Yusupov Collection), who is represented in the Hermitage by six works altogether.

The gallery's collection of eighteenth-century history paintings has been greatly expanded. Natoire's work—previously represented in the Hermitage by only one relatively small work on a mythological subject—can now be studied in several large decorative canvases: the most interesting of these are *The Rape of Europe* and two history paintings with subjects taken from the life of Telemachus. A third work in the series was transferred to the State Museum of Fine Arts in Moscow. Natoire's pictures had been brought to Russia by the art dealer Negri, midway through the nineteenth century. They were purchased from him by Count Vorontsov-Dashkov, whose collection was taken over by the Hermitage after the Revolution. Other post-revolutionary acquisitions were C. A. Coypel's interesting *The Anger of Achilles* (acquired with the P. Durnovo Collection in 1920), Jean Restout's *Juno at the House of Aeolus* (from the Yusupov Collection), and several works by Carle Vanloo.

To the French eighteenth-century portraits were added Nattier's *Portrait of a Lady in Grey* (1920) and *Portrait of Prince A. B. Kurakin* (1923), Carl Vanloo's *Portrait of Abbé Prévost*, and J. B. Vanloo's *Portrait of the Marquis de Prie*. A 1929 addition was the *Portrait of François de Lovat*, a splendid example of Oudry's portraiture, and the most recent acquisition is the *Portrait of a Woman* by F. Drouais, acquired in 1960, which is the first picture by this artist in the Hermitage. The remarkable still-life *The Leg of Veal* by Oudry, which was acquired by the Hermitage in 1923, shows this artist at his best. Of the thirteen Greuzes in the gallery, nine were acquired after the Revolution. These include the *Little Girl with a Doll* from the Academy of Fine Arts and the *Portrait of Countess Catherine Shuvalov* and *The Spoilt Child* from the Paskevich Collection. Unfortunately the works of Fragonard were extremely rare in Russian collections; to the two previous Fragonards in the Hermitage was added *The Snatched Kiss* (plate 81) from the Yusupov Collection, a work remarkable for its free brushwork.

It has already been pointed out that the work of J. Vernet and Hubert Robert enjoyed great popularity in Russia. Of the twenty-five Vernets in the Hermitage, twelve were acquired after the Revolution; and of the fifty works by Robert, only five were in the gallery before 1917. Post-revolutionary acquisitions included some works by artists working in Russia at the turn of the century—G. F. Doyen, Elisabeth L. Vigée-Lebrun, Voille and Mosnier.

The exhibition of French painting from the fifteenth to the twentieth centuries, drawn from the Hermitage and the State Museum in Moscow, opened in Moscow in 1955 and later moved to the Hermitage. It was a remarkably complete and penetrating review of the development of French painting. Many of the pictures from the exhibition were reproduced by Charles Sterling in the second volume of a book on the Hermitage published by the French firm Cercle d'Art in 1957. A detailed catalogue of French painting from the fifteenth to the twentieth centuries in the Hermitage is in preparation.

Outside Germany, Austria and the other countries which had close ties with Germany in the past (Hungary, Poland, the Czech lands and Slovakia), German art of the seventeenth and eighteenth centuries is poorly represented. The Hermitage has more than a hundred pictures by German and Austrian artists, so that its collection compares very well with that of other European galleries. In spite of certain gaps (there are no monumental decorative works by the South German and Austrian masters of the Baroque) it covers the chief trends of these schools.

At the beginning of the eighteenth century cultural relations between Russia and Germany became closer, and the first works by German masters arrived in Russia. A more pronounced interest in German painting, however, was not to be observed until the 1770s and the 1780s, when attention was centred primarily on the neo-classic painters working in Rome. The collections of the two German art-lovers Brühl and Gotzkowski were rich in German works. From them the Hermitage acquired its paintings by Adam Elsheimer and his school, the mythological compositions by Rottenhammer, landscapes by J. H. Roos and his son Philip P. Roos, who was known as Rosa da Tivoli, a landscape by the Dresden painter Thiele (until 1926 in Gatchina Palace), and several pictures by Christian Wilhelm Ernst Dietrich. Elsheimer, who had spent most of his life in Rome and influenced several Dutch

artists, was one of the few German masters who enjoyed popularity outside Germany. Another was Johann Rottenhammer, who lived in Venice.

Russian collectors of the eighteenth century favoured the animal pictures by Rosa da Tivoli, the masterly detailed portraits of aged faces by Balthasar Denner, and the clever imitations of other masters' styles by Christian Dietrich. All these artists were amply represented in Russian private collections, palace galleries, and in the Academy of Art in St Petersburg. Most of these paintings came to the Hermitage after the Revolution. Other popular German artists were Rugendas and Querfurt with their battle-scenes, and Ridinger who specialized in hunting scenes.

Attention soon turned to the Viennese artist J. G. Platzer. During his lifetime his works were brought to Russia first in 1746 and again in 1761, when I. I. Shuvalov acquired fourteen pictures. Platzer was admired for his meticulous craftsmanship which recalled painting on porcelain, as well as for the erotic content of most of his subjects.

But we do not know how other, far more significant works by then little-known German artists were brought to Russia as early as the eighteenth century. These included two works by Christopher Paudiss, of which the *Still-Life* (plate 86) is especially notable, and two versions of *The Rape of the Sabine Women* by Johann Heinrich Schönfeld. Paudiss's work must have attracted attention because it is so close to the work of the Dutch school, and Schönfeld's paintings are very Venetian. A third picture by Schönfeld, *The Wedding in Cana*, came to the Hermitage from a private collection in 1924.

Russian collectors became interested in the German painters who lived in Rome, notably in Mengs. A decisive step was taken by I. I. Shuvalov, who lived in Rome between 1767 and 1773. While there he established friendly relations with many artists and authorities on antique art, including Winckelmann's friend, Johann Friedrich Reiffenstein. Reiffenstein, who was an amateur archaeologist and expert on ancient Rome, was approached by anyone eager to study the monuments of the Eternal City. He was also a close friend of the painters Angelica Kauffmann and J. P. Hackert. Reiffenstein was authorized to supervise students sent to Rome on scholarship grants by the Academy in St Petersburg. He had been recommended to Catherine II as a commissioner by Shuvalov. Winckelmann called Mengs 'the greatest painter of his own and future time', but St Petersburg was slow to recognize Mengs, and it was not until 1776 that Catherine first wished to acquire any of his paintings. By then Mengs had moved to Spain and it was only in 1778 that Reiffenstein commissioned two canvases on themes from the *Iliad*. The pictures were never painted, however, because Mengs, who was busy at the time both with other commissions and with the study of antique monuments, died during the following year. None the less, Reiffenstein arranged for the purchase of Mengs's famous picture *Perseus and Andromeda* dated 1777, and other works were acquired from his heirs, including *St John the Baptist preaching in the Desert*, *The Annunciation*, *The Judgement of Paris*, the sketch *The Descent of the Holy Spirit on the Apostles* and his *Self-Portrait* (plate 89).

The landscape painter J. P. Hackert had been approached even earlier than Mengs. When Shuvalov was charged in 1771 to commission from one of the painters then living in Rome two pictures commemorating the victory of the Russian fleet over the Turks at Chessma, his choice fell on Hackert. But Hackert executed a series of twelve epic canvases on the theme, instead of the two ordered. Goethe describes the origins of the series in his biography of Hackert. The Russian rulers, Catherine II and Paul I, tried repeatedly to lure Hackert to St Petersburg, but he always refused to come. He painted some twenty pictures for Russia, most of which were ordered not for the Hermitage but for the imperial palaces. His pictures include views of the Roman Campagna, the Bay of Naples and Sicily. All the eight Hackert landscapes in the Hermitage were acquired after the Revolution.

In 1782 Reiffenstein commissioned from Angelica Kauffmann the painting *Achilles with the Daughters of King Lycomedes*. The Empress was so delighted with the picture that N. B. Yusupov arranged for the commission of a further work. Two works by the artist on the theme of Sterne's *Sentimental Journey* were bought for the gallery, and other pictures for the palace in Pavlovsk, for the Academy and for Yusupov's collection. The Hermitage now has eleven works by Angelica Kauffmann.

Three Austrian portrait painters were active in Russia during the 1790s. They were L. Guttenbrunn, I. Kreutzinger and J. B. Lampi the Elder, who was the most popular. Lampi painted the portraits of the Empress and most members of her court— Prince A. A. Bezborodko, Count A. I. Mussin-Pushkin, Prince N. B. Yusupov, and a number of others. All these portraits came to the Hermitage after the Revolution, together with other works by Lampi. Several Russian noblemen had their portraits painted on journeys abrod. Before 1917 only one example was in the Hermitage, a painting by J. Grassi, acquired in 1900. The number was increased during the post-revolutionary years to two portraits by Grassi, two by J. F. A. Tischbein and three by A. Graff.

Very few additions were made to the German collection during the nineteenth century. In 1814 a sketch for the fresco *Parnassus* by Mengs was bought in Paris, and in 1823 the *Family Portrait* by J. Ovens ascribed to Van Dyck was acquired from the Russian collection. Collectors of the late-nineteenth and twentieth centuries lost all interest in that period of German painting, so that the works which trickled into their collections were bought in the mistaken belief that they were Dutch paintings. In this way Ovens's interesting *Self-Portrait* was thought to be a van der Helst, and entered the Hermitage with the well-known Semyonov-Tianshansky Collection of Dutch art in 1915. The *Adoration of the Shepherds* by the Hamburg artist M. Scheits, who studied in the Netherlands, and a battle-scene by J. Weyer entered the Hermitage with the same collection.

Only after the Revolution did the Hermitage begin to round out its collection of German and Austrian baroque and classical painting. Among the paintings acquired in this time was *Portrait of a Mongolian Merchant with his Family* (plate 87) by D. Schulz, who worked in Danzig. Until 1937 the work was in the picture gallery at Tsarskoe Selo. Other works recently acquired by the Hermitage include two still-lifes by the Frankfurt artist Georg Flegel, who has only recently been studied more closely, a still-life by Franz Werner Tamm, the large

Allegory of Peace, Art and Abundance by Hans von Aachen—who was court painter to Rudolf II—and finally *Tobias* by Karl Andreas Ruthart, who is better known as a painter of animals. The well-known history painting, *Conrad of Swabia before his Execution*, by Wilhelm Tischbein, two landscapes by Johann Friedrich Weitsch, and two works by Johann Conrad Seekatz, which only recently have been identified, are the most notable paintings by German eighteenth-century artists in the collection.

N. B. Yusupov and A. S. Stroganov each bought one picture by the German painter Füger. Yusupov had his portrait painted by him, and today five works by Füger hang in the Hermitage.

Thanks to constant efforts to extend the German and Austrian collections in the Hermitage, there are now three large rooms of German painting and one of Austrian in the gallery.

The collection of English painting in the Hermitage is neither very large nor representative of the best work of that school. The gallery has however pictures by the most important eighteenth-century masters, as well as a few by sixteenth, seventeenth and early nineteenth-century artists. The English paintings in the Hermitage were collected as early as the eighteenth century—this is earlier than in most other European galleries. The Louvre, for example, and the German art galleries did not begin to collect English pictures until the beginning of this century.

The diplomat Lord Carysfort, through whom the Empress Catherine and Prince Potemkin commissioned paintings from Reynolds, asserted that he was instrumental in getting the works of English painters into Russian collections. In a letter to Sir Joshua Reynolds dated December 8th, 1785, he wrote: 'Since I am not one of those people who are ashamed to admit their love of their country and everything about it, I have expressed my regret at every visit to the Hermitage that the gallery should not have a single example of the work of the painters of the English school. I am proud to say that I turned Her Majesty's attention to our painters'. But Lord Carysfort slightly overestimated his services, for there were some English

works in the Hermitage at that time. As early as 1774, Joseph Wright had been commissioned to paint *The Forge* (plate 93), one of the works on the theme of crafts and trades that are so prominent in this artist's work. The Russians may have interested themselves in Wright, who was not too well known at that time, because he had taken up residence in Rome. Two further works were bought from Wright, both painted during his second stay in Italy, *Fireworks at Castel S. Angelo* and *Mount Vesuvius Erupting* (now in the State Museum of Fine Arts in Moscow). This popular theme was also painted by several other artists living in Rome, including the Frenchman Volaire and the German J. P. Hackert, who painted *The Eruption of Etna* for the Empress Catherine. At the same time as the Hermitage acquired the works by Wright it also purchased several more English pictures with the Walpole Collection. This collection had two portraits by the greatest English master of the late seventeenth century, Godfrey Kneller—the *Portrait of the Sculptor Grinling Gibbons* and the *Portrait of John Locke*, and also Dobson's *Portrait of the Painter van der Dort*. The portrait gallery of European monarchs in the summer residence included three official court portraits by Benjamin West dated 1778 (these were transferred to the Hermitage from Peterhof in 1931).

Russia established closer contact with English art in the following years. In 1779 the great Scottish architect Charles Cameron settled in Russia, and designed buildings in Tsarskoe Selo and Pavlovsk. When the Russian architect V. Nieyelov returned home from a trip to England in 1778, he brought with him a large collection of engravings of English country houses which was kept in one of the 'gothic' pavilions which he had designed in the palace grounds in Tsarskoe Selo. Many English country houses decorated the famous 'green Frog dinner service' ordered from Wedgwood in the early seventies. The British Ambassador Charles Williams in one of his letters of 1779 referred to Catherine as 'an admirer and partisan of the English way of laying out parks'.

Towards the close of the eighteenth century the Hermitage had an excellent collection of English engravings, which were sold in St Petersburg bookshops and art shops. Besides the

Walpole Collection another large collection was bought between 1783 and 1787, the Lyde Brown Collection of antique sculpture. This was taken to Tsarskoe Selo, where it remained until it was transferred to the Hermitage in the middle of the nineteenth century to form the basis of the museum's collection of antique sculpture.

From what we have said now about the interest of Russian connoisseurs in English art, there can be no surprise that paintings were commissioned from Sir Joshua Reynolds. From letters which have survived, we are well informed about the circumstances of that commission. Reynolds painted a picture on a subject of his own choice, *The Infant Hercules strangles the Snakes*. The following year he painted *The Continence of Scipio* for Potemkin. Both works were exhibited at the Royal Academy in London in 1788 and 1789, before being shipped to Russia. In 1786 Sir Joshua was commissioned to paint a replica of his *Cupid untying the Girdle of Venus* (plate 91), the earliest version of which is in the National Gallery, London. He finished this in 1791. He also sent a copy of his *Discourses* to the Empress. Catherine read the book, as she herself wrote, eagerly, and appreciated its well-written deliberations on art and artists. She declared it to be one of the best books of its kind and had the Russian translation published in St Petersburg in 1790.

Unfortunately, the Hermitage has none of Reynolds's portraits. His only 'Russian' portrait, that of Prince Serge Gagarin and his wife and son, is lost and known merely from an engraving published in London in 1785.

The only English portrait painter to work in Russia was the unimaginative and dry Richard Brompton. When he died in 1782 the Russian Ambassador to England tried to invite some other English artist to Russia. From documents published in recent years we know that negotiations went on with Sir Joshua Reynolds to try to persuade either of the young and gifted portrait painters John Hoppner and Thomas Lawrence to accept the invitation, but nothing came of the attempt.

The English collection in the Hermitage acquired only two more works in those years, the *Landscape with Aeneas and Dido*, the finest work of Thomas Jones, a minor but not ungifted artist, and the *Seashore* by William Marlowe.

During the whole nineteenth century the English collection remained unchanged. Only in 1916 from the legacy of A. Z. Khitrovo—the only Russian collector interested in English eighteenth-century painting—came seven portraits, including Gainsborough's *Portrait of the Duchess of Beaufort* (plate 92). The unerring taste of Khitrovo ensured that the remaining six works—by Romney, Raeburn, Hoppner, Opie and Thomas Lawrence—were of an equally high order. The Hermitage acquired at the same time two more portraits— the *Portrait of Count S. R. Vorontsov*, attributed to Romney, and a *Portrait of J. Rogers* by the little-known painter James Saxon. Since there were few English works in Russian private collections, no important acquisitions were made by the Hermitage after the Revolution. The only exceptions were six pictures by George Morland (obtained between 1919 and 1925), which show the qualities of his landscape and genre paintings, a small work by F. Wheatley, *The Infatuated Huntsman*, a mythological composition by Benjamin West (from the Yusupov Collection), and the *Portrait of Sir Benjamin Bathurst*, by J. B. Clostermann, which dates from the close of the seventeenth century. In more recent years a few works by nineteenth-century artists have been acquired, notably the exquisite *Portrait of Count M. S. Vorontsov* by Sir Thomas Lawrence. This is the only full-length portrait in the Hermitage's English collection.

LIST OF ILLUSTRATIONS

LIST OF ABBREVIATIONS

Cat. 1900
*Imperatorsky Ermitazh. Katalog kartinnoy gale-
rey. Sostavil A. Somov. No. III. Angliiskaya
i frantsuskaya zhivopis*, Saint Petersburg, 1900.

Cat. 1903
*Ermitage impérial. Catalogue de la galerie des
tableaux. Troisième partie. École anglaise et école
française*, A. Somov, St Petersburg, 1903.

Cat. 1912
*Imperatorsky Ermitazh. Katalog kartinnoy gale-
rey. C. I. Italyanskaya i ispanskaya zhivopis*,
Saint Petersburg, 1912.

Cat. 1916
*Imperatorsky Ermitazh. Kratky katalog kartinnoy
galerey*, Petrograd, 1916.

Cat. 1958
*Gosudarstvenny Ermitazh. Otdel zapadnoevro-
peiskogo isskustva. Katalog zhivopisi I, II*, V. F.
Levinson-Lessing, Leningrad–Moskva, 1958.

Aedes Valpolianae
*Aedes Walpolianae. Descriptions of the Collection
of Pictures at Houghton Hall in Norfolk*, London,
1767.

Chefs d'œuvre
*Chefs d'œuvre de l'art français du XVIIIᵉ siècle.
Palais National des Arts. Catalogue*, Paris, 1937.

Réau
L. Réau, *Catalogue de l'art français dans les
musées russes*, Paris, 1929.

PLATES

MICHELANGELO MERISI
DA CARAVAGGIO
(1573–1610)

THE LUTE PLAYER
oil on canvas, 94 × 119 cm

The Lute Player is one of the best works of Caravaggio's early period. It may have been painted *c.* 1595 in Rome for the Cardinal Francesco del Monte. At the same time Caravaggio also painted *The Concert* (Metropolitan Museum of Art, New York), which is close to *The Lute Player* both in its subject and its format. But according to the recent suggestion of S. Borla, both pictures were painted by the master while he was still in Milan, and subsequently taken to Rome.

The Lute Player was painted from the same model as the *Boy bitten by a Lizard* (R. Longhi Collection, Florence), *The Concert* (New York), and a few other canvases. It shows a black-haired youth with softly rounded, somewhat feminine features (which led some specialists to suppose that the lute player was a young girl). S. Borla suggested that the word inscribed on the music book, for which the reading of 'Bassus' had been generally accepted, was really 'Gallus'. Gallus was the name of a young Milanese musician, a friend of Caravaggio; the new reading would identify the sitter as Gallus.

A few years ago, the notation in the music-book lying open in front of the lute player, was read, and the tune was identified as the popular sixteenth-century madrigal by Jacques Arcadelt 'Voi sapete ch' io v'amo' (published by G. Bazin).

The picture became part of the Giustiniani Collection in Rome, and in 1808 when the collection arrived in Paris, was purchased for the Hermitage.

Literature:
Cat. 1912, pp. 99–100, No 217; Cat. 1958, I, p. 103, No 45; Giov. Baglione, *Vite de' Pittori, Scultori ed Architetti*, Rome, 1652, p. 136; G. P. Bellori, *Vite de' Pittori, Scultori ed Architetti*, Rome, 1672, p. 202; L. Venturi, 'Studi su Michelangelo de Caravaggio', *L'arte*, 1910, pp. 197, 198; H. Voss, 'Caravaggios Frühzeit', *Jahrbuch der Preussischen Kunstsammlungen*, 1923, pp. 78–80; L. Zahn, *Caravaggio*, Berlin, 1928, pp. 11, 34, 35; D. Mahon, 'Addenda to Caravaggio', *The Burlington Magazine*, 1952 (January), pp. 4, 8; W. Friedländer, *Caravaggio Studies*, Princeton, 1955, pp. 155, 156; G. Bazin, *Les grands maîtres de la peinture à l'Ermitage*, Paris, 1958, pp. 67–70; S. Borla, 'Opere milanesi del Caravaggio', *Emporium*, 1963 (October).

2 MICHELANGELO MERISI
DA CARAVAGGIO
(1573–1610)

THE LUTE PLAYER
(Detail)

3 ANNIBALE CARRACCI
   (1560–1609)

REST ON THE FLIGHT INTO EGYPT
oil on canvas; tondo, diam. 82.5 cm

The *Rest on the Flight into Egypt* is one of the best classical landscapes by Annibale Carracci. It was painted in Rome *c.* 1600 and shows an ideal image of nature, unchangeable and eternal, conceived in the artist's mind and executed in strict accordance with the classical canon of beauty. This type of landscape was practised by the painters of the academic school, and achieved its culmination in the landscapes of the French masters Nicolas Poussin and Claude Lorrain. Classical landscapes were generally animated with groups of figures illustrating subjects taken from the Bible or from Greek and Roman mythology.

Acquired for the Hermitage in 1772 with the Crozat Collection, Paris.

Literature:
Cat. 1912, p. 102, No 171; Cat. 1958, I, p. 106, No 138; G. Rouchés, 'La peinture bolonaise à la fin du XVIe siècle', *Les Carrache*, Paris, 1913, p. 134; G. Rouchés, 'Le paysage chez les peintres de l'école bolonaise', *Gazette des Beaux-Arts*, 1921 (January), p. 18; S. N. Vsevolozhskaya, I. S. Grigoryeva, T. D. Fomicheva, *Italyanskaya zhivopis XIII–XVIII vekov v sobranii Ermitazha*, Leningrad, 1964, pp. 249, 301.

4   ANNIBALE CARRACCI
(1560–1609)

REST ON THE FLIGHT INTO EGYPT
(Detail)

5 ANNIBALE CARRACCI
(1560–1609)

THE THREE MARYS AT THE TOMB
oil on canvas, 121 × 145.5 cm

The Hermitage picture, which was painted *c.* 1605, is one of the masterpieces of Annibale Carracci's late period. The palette, which is restricted to a range of cool tones, with bright local colours and dark shadows, is typical of this period of the master's production. A painting in the St Louis Art Gallery, ascribed to A. Carracci, is close to the Hermitage picture.

The picture illustrates an episode from the Gospels which tells how the three Marys came to Christ's sepulchre and found it open, and an angel in it who told them of the resurrection of Christ (Mark XVI, 1–7).

The work was painted for Signor Pasqualino, from whom it passed to Cardinal Agucchi. On his death the canvas became part of the collection of Cardinal Filomarino, Archbishop of Naples: it was next owned by the Duke della Torre, the nephew of Filomarino. In the eighteenth century the picture was in the Palazzo della Torre in Naples; in the early part of the nineteenth century it entered the collection of Lucien Bonaparte. It was later acquired by N. G. Coesvelt and brought to London whence it came to the Hermitage in 1836.

Literature:
Cat. 1912, p. 103, No 173; Cat. 1958, I, p. 106, No 92; C. C. Malvasia, *Felsina pittrice*, 1678, I, p. 501; H. Voss, *Die Malerei des Barock in Rom*, Berlin, 1924, p. 502; D. Mahon, *Studies in Seicento Art and Theory*, London, 1947, pp. 73, 74; S. N. Vsevolozhskaya, I. S. Grigoryeva, T. D. Fomicheva, *Italyanskaya zhivopis XIII–XVIII vekov v sobranii Ermitazha*, Leningrad, 1964, pp. 250, 301.

6   GUIDO RENI
(1575–1642)

THE BUILDING OF NOAH'S ARK
oil on canvas, 193.5 × 154.5 cm

The subject is taken from the Bible. Following the command of God, Noah and his sons built a ship which was called an ark, in which they saved themselves from the Flood (Genesis VI, 14–22). The choice of subject is unusual.

The picture came to the Hermitage as a Domenichino and was catalogued as such until 1860 when it was re-attributed and described as the work of an unknown master of the Bolognese school of the seventeenth century. In 1911 it was again attributed to Domenichino because it was thought to be close to his fresco *The Building of a Monastery* at Grottaferrata near Rome. In 1956 M. I. Shcherbacheva established the authorship of Guido Reni. The work is very close to Reni's paintings of the first decade of the seventeenth century, when there was a marked Caravaggesque influence on Reni. It was probably painted in 1608 when Guido Reni and Domenichino were both engaged in the decoration of the Church of San Gregorio Magno in Rome.

Acquired for the Hermitage in 1769 with the Brühl Collection, Dresden.

Literature:
Cat. 1912, p. 91, No 212 (Domenichino); Cat. 1958, I, p. 161, No 51 (Guido Reni); E. Liphart, 'Priobreteniya i pereveski', *Starye Gody*, 1910 (January–March), p. 14; M. Shcherbacheva, 'Kartiny Guido Reni v sobranii Ermitazha', *Trudy Gosudarstvennogo Ermitazha*, 1956, I, pp. 73–80; S. N. Vsevolozhskaya, I. S. Grigoryeva, T. D. Fomicheva, *Italyanskaya zhivopis XIII–XVIII vekov v sobranii Ermitazha*, Leningrad, 1964, pp. 250, 251, 301.

7   GUERCINO
    (GIOVANNI FRANCESCO BARBIERI)
    (1591–1666)

THE VISION OF ST CLARE
oil on canvas, 50×37.5 cm

The picture illustrates a religious subject. It shows
the Virgin and Child appearing in a vision to St
Clare of Assisi (1193–1243; canonized in 1255).
Some art-historians have in the past doubted the
attribution to Guercino; they thought that the
painting was closer to Schedone. But the work has
been firmly attributed to Guercino, and dated to
the early part of his career. It is painted in warm
dark colours, with the strong contrasts of light and
shade which are characteristic of Guercino's painting during the period 1615–1621.
Two replicas of the composition are known: one
in the R. Longhi Collection, Florence; the other,
in the Museum of Angers (both called *The Vision
of St Francesca*). The Zanetti Collection had a drawing which was closely related in composition to
The Vision of St Clare.

There is some evidence that the picture may once
have formed part of the Tugni Collection, Paris;
later it was owned by the Duc de Tallard, Paris;
then it entered the Crozat Collection, with which
it came to the Hermitage in 1772.

Literature:
Cat. 1912, p. 83, No 243; Cat. 1958, I, p. 84, No
156; S. N. Vsevolozhskaya, I. S. Grigoryeva, T. D.
Fomicheva, *Italyanskaya zhivopis XIII–XVIII vekov
v sobranii Ermitazha*, Leningrad, 1964, pp. 253, 254,
301.

8 **CARLO DOLCI**
(1616–1686)

ST CATHERINE
oil on canvas, 115.5 × 92 cm

The *St Catherine* is one of Dolci's best-known and most popular pictures. The colours are characteristically dark, and somewhat gaudy. The details are finely executed, in spite of a certain dryness in some of the drawing. The head and face of St Catherine, which is modelled in soft shadows, is the most attractive part of the painting.
Dolci's works are distinguished by a brilliant virtuosity of technique, and a studied elegance which is typical of the Florentine school of painting. They were very popular in his own day.

Acquired for the Hermitage in 1814 with the collection of the Empress Josephine at Malmaison.

Literature:
Cat. 1912, p. 89, No 254; Cat. 1958, I, p. 95, No 46.

9 DOMENICO FETTI
(1589–1623)

PORTRAIT OF AN ACTOR
oil on canvas, 105.5×81 cm

The *Portrait of an Actor* is one of the master's best paintings; it is an excellent example of Italian seventeenth-century portraiture. The picture probably dates from the last period of Fetti's career, the early 1620s, when the artist was strongly influenced by Venetian sixteenth-century painting. The *Portrait of an Actor* is remarkable both for its depth of psychological characterization and for its brilliant technique and harmonious colours.

The portrait was long supposed to represent the actor Giovanni Gabrielli (otherwise known as Sivello). Some authorities, however, identified the sitter as Duke Ferdinando Gonzaga; and it was even suggested that the person represented was none other than Don Quixote. The most plausible suggestion, in our opinion, is that the master has here portrayed Tristano Martinelli (d. 1630 or 1631), an actor in the company at Mantua, who was widely celebrated in Italy and France for his assumption of the role of Harlequin.

The picture now in the Hermitage is known to have been in the collection of Cardinal Mazarini: later it formed part of the Crozat Collection, and in 1772 was acquired for the Hermitage.

Literature:
Cat. 1912, p. 198, No 236; Cat. 1958, I, p. 202, No 153; E. K. Liphart, 'Priobreteniya i pereveski', *Starye Gody*, 1910 (January), p. 13; G. Fiocco, *Venetian Painting of the Seicento and the Settecento*, New York, p. 17; F. J. Mather, *Venetian Painting*, London, 1937, p. 432; S. N. Vsevolozhskaya, I. S. Grigoryeva, T. D. Fomicheva, *Italyanskaya zhivopis XIII–XVIII vekov v sobranii Ermitazha*, Leningrad, 1964, pp. 261, 302.

BERNARDO STROZZI
(1581–1644)

TOBIAS HEALING HIS FATHER
oil on canvas, 158 × 223.5 cm

The picture illustrates an episode from the Book of
Tobit. The young Tobias heals the blindness of his
father Tobit with the bile of the fish which he has
caught (Tobit II, 13–15).
The work was painted by Strozzi soon after his
arrival in Venice, probably *c.* 1635. It shows the
combined influences of Caravaggio and of the Venetian masters of the Cinquecento. The painter's
debt to Caravaggio is evident in the composition,
and in the use of peasant types, while the rich palette of light colours, and the freedom of the handling mark the influence of the Venetian school. The
figure of Tobit's wife is reminiscent of one of the
Fates in *The Three Fates* (the Pelliccioli Collection,
Milan), also dating from the 1630s.
There are several versions of *Tobias healing his
Father*. The picture in the Church of San Zaccaria,
Venice, is closest to the Hermitage canvas.

Acquired for the Hermitage before 1774.

Literature:
Cat. 1912, p. 184; No 219; Cat. 1958, I, p. 185,
No 16. A. Vasilchikov, 'Novye priobretenia imperatorskogo Ermitazha', *Vestnik iziashchnykh iskusstv*,
1883, I, p. 23; G. Fiocco, *La pittura veneziana del
Seicento e del Settecento*, Verona, 1929, p. 21; S. N.
Vsevolozhskaya, I. S. Grigoryeva, T. D. Fomicheva, *Italyanskaya zhivopis XIII–XVIII vekov v sobranii Ermitazha*, Leningrad, 1964, pp. 269, 302.

11 CARLO MARATTA
(1625–1713)

PORTRAIT OF POPE CLEMENT IX
oil on canvas, 158 × 118.5 cm

Signed on the sheet of paper on the table: *Alla Santita di N. Sig. re Clemente IX per Carlo Maratta.*

The picture is a fine example of seventeenth-century formal portraiture, and one of the best of Maratta's portraits. Clement IX (1600–1669) came from the house of the Rospigliosi; he became Pope in 1667. Bellori, the biographer of Maratta, states that the portrait was painted in the Palazzo di Sabina, in the Pope's lifetime. Two signed versions of the portrait are known, which are close to one another; one is the Hermitage canvas, and the other is in the Vatican. Until quite recently it was not clear which of the two canvases was the version mentioned by Bellori. But the last restoration of the Hermitage picture revealed an inscription on the sheet of paper lying on the table, which reads *Alla Santita di N. Sig. re Clemente IX per Carlo Maratta* ('To His Holiness Pope Clement IX from Carlo Maratta'). The dedicatory inscription shows that the portrait is datable to the Pope's lifetime, and is, consequently, the one described by Bellori. There are a number of replicas and copies of the painting.

There is some evidence that the Hermitage picture once formed part of the Pallavicini Collection (Palazzo Rospigliosi, Rome); it was later in the Arnaldi Palace, then came into the hands of Pater Gervasio, and lastly entered the Walpole Collection, with which it came to the Hermitage in 1779.

Literature:
Cat. 1912, p. 127, No 307; Cat. 1958, I, p. 132, No 42; G. P. Bellori, *Vita di Carlo Maratta*, Rome, 1732, pp. 23–26; W. Bode, *Kaiserliche Gemälde Galerie der Ermitage in St Petersburg*, VII, Berlin, 1882, p. 9, No 307; H. Voss, *Die Malerei des Barock im Rom*, Berlin, 1924, p. 599; K. M. Malitskaya, 'K probleme realizma v ispanskom iskusstve XVII veka', *Trudy Gosudarstvennogo muzeya izobrazitelnykh iskusstv im. Pushkina*, Moscow-Leningrad, 1939, pp. 64, 65; S. N. Vsevolozhskaya, I. S. Grigoryeva, T. D. Fomicheva, *Italyanskaya zhivopis XIII–XVIII vv. v sobranii Ermitazha*, Leningrad, 1964, pp. 265, 302.

SALVATOR ROSA
(1615–1673)

PORTRAIT OF A MAN
oil on canvas, 78×64.5 cm

The picture has been called *The Italian Robber, The Brigand Captain* and *Portrait of a Brigand*. There is also a suggestion that the work is a self-portrait. It is probably the self-portrait which Salvator Rosa painted for the Florentine Girolamo Signoretti and which was later owned by Cardinal Leopold of Tuscany. This is mentioned by Baldinucci, who says that Salvator Rosa painted himself in the costume of Pascariello, a character in the Italian Commedia dell' Arte. Of all the surviving works by the master, the Hermitage picture is closest to this description. The frontal and somewhat rigid pose, the gaze directed straight at the viewer, suggest that it may well be a self-portrait painted in front of a mirror. The features of the face are very like those of many other characters in pictures by Rosa which are also self-portraits. The painting closest to the Hermitage picture is the canvas in the Uffizi known as *La Menzogna* ('The Lie'). The two pictures were both painted in the 1640s, when Salvator Rosa was working in Florence.

Acquired for the Hermitage in 1779 with the Walpole Collection from Houghton Hall, Norfolk, England.

Literature:
Cat. 1912, p. 171, No 225; Cat. 1958, I, p. 166, No 1483; F. Baldinucci, *Notizie de' Professori del disegno da Cimabue in quà*, Florence, 1773, XIX, p. 27; L. Ozzola, *Vita e opere di Salvator Rosa*, Strasbourg, 1908, pp. 95, 96; H. Voss, *Die Malerei des Barock in Rom*, Berlin, 1924, p. 572; S. N. Vsevolozhskaya, I. S. Grigoryeva, T. D. Fomicheva, *Italyanskaya zhivopis XIII–XVIII vekov v sobranii Ermitazha*, Leningrad, 1964, pp. 273, 302.

13 LUCA GIORDANO
    (1632–1705)

THE FORGE OF VULCAN
oil on canvas (transferred from a panel),
192.5 × 151.5 cm

This is one of Giordano's early paintings. It is an
outstanding work, broadly painted and perfectly
drawn. The prevailing tonality is a beautiful silver
grey. Chiaroscuro is used with masterly skill.
The subject of the picture is taken from Virgil's
Aeneid (Book VIII, 424–453). The scene is set in the
forge of Vulcan, the god of fire, where cyclopes
forge lightning for Jupiter the Thunderer. Giordano painted other versions of this theme, including the canvases now in the galleries of Graz and
Pesaro. A copy of the Hermitage painting, executed
by Walton, was in St James's Palace in London in
the eighteenth century.

The Hermitage picture was in the collection of the
sculptor Grinling Gibbons in the early eighteenth
century, then in the Walpole Collection at Houghton Hall, Norfolk. It was acquired for the Hermitage in 1779.

Literature:
Cat. 1912, p. 85, No 1638; Cat. 1958, I, p. 91, No
188; S. N. Vsevolozhskaya, I. S. Grigoryeva, T. D.
Fomicheva, *Italyanskaya zhivopis XIII–XVIII vekov
v sobranii Ermitazha*, Leningrad, 1964, pp. 276, 303.

14 FRANCESCO SOLIMENA
(1657–1747)

REBECCA AT THE WELL
oil on canvas, 72×63 cm

The subject is taken from an episode in the Old Testament. Eliezer, the servant of Abraham, was sent to the neighbouring country to find a wife for Isaac; he meets Rebecca at the well, and she gives him and his camels water to drink. Eliezer chooses her as a wife for Isaac (Genesis XXIV, 15–22). The picture is painted with broad, free brush-strokes, in a beautiful colour scheme of light and dark shades of blue, with bright reds and yellows. The handling of light and shade is masterly, as is the modelling of the figures.

In Bernardo de Dominici's lives of the Neapolitan painters, two pictures of this subject are mentioned: one at Casa Baglione; the other painted for Aghir, who presented it to King Philip V of Spain. Several pictures of this subject, almost identical in composition, are known besides the version in the Hermitage: these include the larger version in the Academy, Venice, another at the York City Museum, England, as well as a number in other collections. It has not yet been established which of these pictures were the ones mentioned by de Dominici.

Transferred to the Hermitage from the Great Peterhof Palace in 1921.

Literature:
Cat. 1958, I, p. 181, No 2; F. Bologna, *Francesco Solimena*, Naples, 1958, p. 277; S. N. Vsevolozhskaya, I. S. Grigoryeva, T. D. Fomicheva, *Italyanskaya zhivopis XIII–XVIII vekov v sobranii Ermitazha*, Leningrad, 1964, pp. 278, 303.

ALESSANDRO MAGNASCO
(1667–1749)

LANDSCAPE WITH SEASHORE
oil on canvas, 158×211 cm

The *Landscape with Seashore* and its companion *Mountain Landscape* (see plate 17) belong to a group of Magnasco's works which create an image of ever-varying, ever-changing nature. Dynamism is the dominant note of these pictures and every detail is given a sense of movement—the trees bent by the wind, the rolling, swirling clouds in the sky, the waves of the sea rising like mountains, and the mountains as restless as the sea. Amidst this grand spectacle of the mighty works of nature, the figures of men appear to be tiny; they are living their own lives, but are still part of the life of nature. In this, as well as in other works by Magnasco, strange, elongated human beings perform simple everyday tasks; the fishermen draw in their nets, the monk reads his book, and the woman does her washing. Both the *Landscape with Seashore* and *Mountain Landscape* are a dark bluish-green in colour, with bright flashes of light. The figures of people are indicated by a few sharp, quick touches of the brush. The pictures date from the mature period of Magnasco's career, the 1720s.

Purchased in 1919 from Prince V. N. Argutinsky-Dolgoruky.

Literature:
Cat. 1958, I, p. 130, No 3527; S. N. Vsevolozhskaya, I. S. Grigoryeva, T. D. Fomicheva, *Italyanskaya zhivopis XIII–XVIII vekov v sobranii Ermitazha*, Leningrad, 1964, pp. 272, 302.

16 ALESSANDRO MAGNASCO
    (1667–1749)

LANDSCAPE WITH SEASHORE
(Detail)

17　ALESSANDRO MAGNASCO
(1667–1749)

MOUNTAIN LANDSCAPE
oil on canvas, 158×211 cm

The *Mountain Landscape*, like its companion the
Landscape with Seashore (see plates 15, 16), was painted in the 1720s.

Purchased in 1919 from Prince V. N. Argutinsky-
Dolgoruky.

Literature:
Cat. 1958, I, p. 130, No 3528; S. N. Vsevolozhskaya, I. S. Grigoryeva, T. D. Fomicheva, *Italyanskaya zhivopis XIII–XVIII vekov v sobranii Ermitazha*, Leningrad, 1964, p. 272.

18 GIUSEPPE MARIA CRESPI
(1664–1747)

THE DEATH OF ST JOSEPH
oil on canvas, 234.5 × 187 cm

The picture shows St Joseph on his deathbed attended by Christ, the Virgin Mary and the archangels Michael and Gabriel (Isidorus Isolanus, *Summa de donis S. Joseph*, Pavia, 1522, IV, IX).
Together with its companion picture *The Holy Family* (State Pushkin Museum of Fine Arts, Moscow), *The Death of St Joseph* was probably painted in 1712. Both works, according to Zanotti, were executed for Cardinal Pietro Ottoboni at Bologna. *The Death of St Joseph* was painted during the period when Crespi's art reached its peak, and ranks among his best works. The subject, which was very popular in Italian seventeenth and eighteenth-century painting, was painted by Crespi several times. Another version, which is very close to the Hermitage painting in composition, is in the Corsini Gallery in Rome.

On the death of Cardinal Ottoboni, *The Death of St Joseph* and *The Holy Family* passed to the Brühl Collection, with which they came to the Hermitage in 1769.

Literature:
Cat. 1912, p. 110, No 314; Cat. 1958, I, p. 114, No 25; V. Lasareff, 'Studies on Giuseppe Maria Crespi', *Art in America*, 1929, p. 18; S. N. Vsevolozhskaya, I. S. Grigoryeva, T. D. Fomicheva, *Italyanskaya zhivopis XIII–XVIII vekov v sobranii Ermitazha*, Leningrad, 1964, pp. 256, 301.

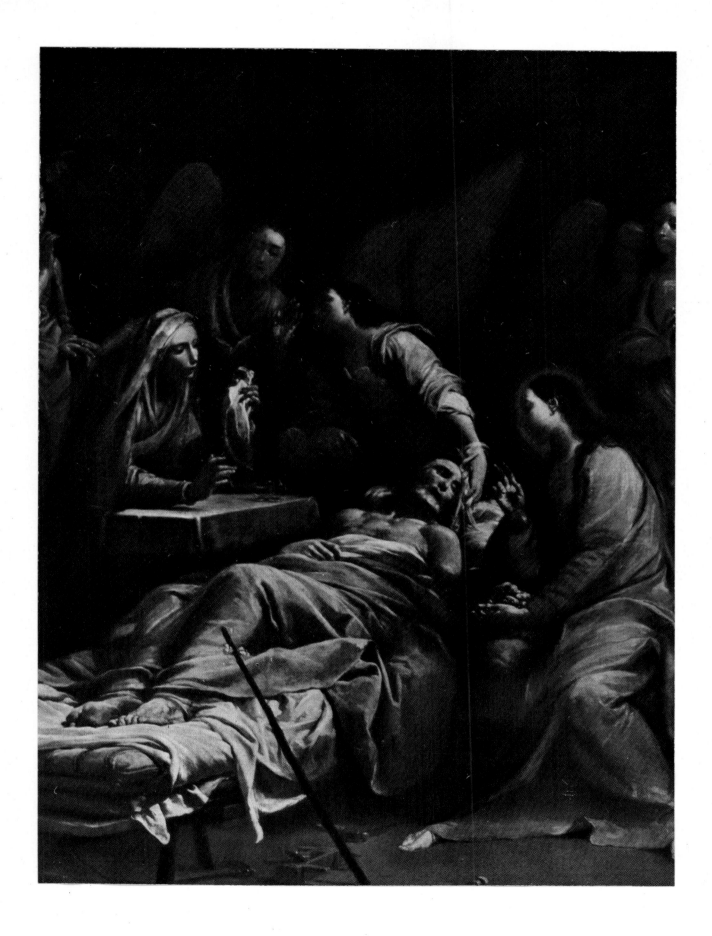

19   GIUSEPPE MARIA CRESPI
     (1664–1747)

SELF-PORTRAIT
oil on canvas, 60.5 × 50 (oval)

The *Self-Portrait* was painted by Crespi with so much directness, vividness and spontaneity that it gives the impression of having been done very quickly, for the artist's own private use. The simplest devices serve to create a vital, expressive picture of a clever, witty man; and Crespi was a Bolognese with a fine sense of humour. The portrait, like the best of Crespi's work, is restrained in colouring, with brownish tones, and is painted in a broad, nervous style.

The picture was painted in 1700 when the artist was just beginning to paint his best pictures.

In the eighteenth century, when the picture was in the Baudouin Collection, it was regarded as a self-portrait by Domenico Fetti; but in the Hermitage catalogues it has always been described as the work of Crespi.

An X-ray of the picture shows that it was painted on old canvas, which had already been used for a different composition: on the left of the earlier picture there is a very beautiful female head which is the same size as the head in our portrait.

Acquired for the Hermitage in 1781 with the Baudouin Collection, Paris.

Literature:
Cat. 1912, p. 111, No 315; Cat. 1958, I, p. 112, No 189; M. Marangoni, 'Giuseppe Maria Crespi detto lo Spagnolo', *Dedalo*, I, 1920–1921, p. 578; S. N. Vsevolozhskaya, I. S. Grigoryeva, T. D. Fomicheva, *Italyanskaya zhivopis XIII–XVIII vekov v sobranii Ermitazha*, Leningrad, 1964, pp. 256, 301.

20

GIUSEPPE MARIA CRESPI
(1664–1747)

THE LAUNDRESS
oil on copper, 25 × 18.5 cm

The Laundress and its companion the *Woman hunting
for Fleas*, also in the Hermitage, date from Crespi's
best period, the 1710s–1720s, when he painted a
number of genre scenes. He also provided illustrations for history books, in which he represented
various genre subjects. Both the pictures under
discussion are quite small in size; but the broad
handling of the painting, the generalized forms and
the absence of small insignificant details lend
dignity to the subject, and give it the monumental
quality which is so characteristic of all Crespi's
paintings.

In the eighteenth century both pictures formed
part of the collection of Prince D. M. Golitsyn,
Russian Ambassador in Vienna; this is known from
the inscriptions on engravings made after the
pictures by I. Feigl in 1775. The inscriptions name
Carlo da Bologna as the author of the pictures;
later they were attributed to Giuseppe Maria Crespi.
In the second half of the nineteenth century they
were owned by A. I. Somov, keeper of the Hermitage Picture Gallery, from whose executors they
were acquired for the Hermitage in 1939.

Literature:
Cat. 1958, I, p. 114, No 9617; M. I. Shcherbacheva, 'Novye kartiny J. M. Crespi v Ermitazhe',
Soobshcheniya Gosudarstvennogo Ermitazha, VI, 1954,
pp. 25, 26.

21

VITTORE GHISLANDI
(FRA GALGARIO)
(1655–1743)

PORTRAIT OF A BOY
oil on canvas, 67 × 52 cm

The *Portrait of a Boy* is one of Ghislandi's late paintings. It is remarkable for the beauty of its fresh,
rich colouring and for the unaffected simplicity and
spontaneity of the treatment of the subject.
Francesco Maria Tassi in his biography of Ghislandi mentions that in 1732 the master sent a
picture showing the head of a boy clothed in magnificent fabrics to the Marquis Andrea Gerini in Florence. The Hermitage *Portrait of a Boy* was acquired
by one of its former owners from a Florentine antiquary who often bought pictures from the collections of the impoverished Florentine aristocracy.
There is every probability that the Hermitage
portrait is the canvas mentioned by Tassi.

Acquired for the Hermitage in 1921 from the collection of L. M. and E. L. Kochubei, Petrograd.

Literature:
Cat. 1958, I, p. 85, No 5560; E. K. Liphart, 'Kar-
tiny v sobranii L. M. i E. L. Kochubei', *Starye
Gody*, 1912 (January-March), p. 24.

22

GIOVANNI BATTISTA TIEPOLO
(1696–1770)

MAECENAS PRESENTING THE LIBERAL ARTS
TO THE EMPEROR AUGUSTUS
oil on canvas, 69.5 × 89 cm

The literature on Tiepolo often gives incorrect information about the date of this picture, the person for whom it was executed, and the date of its acquisition by the Hermitage. It is obvious from the correspondence of Count Algarotti that the work was ordered from Tiepolo by Algarotti in 1743. It was intended for Count Brühl. The building seen in the distance represents Count Brühl's palace. The picture shows the Emperor Augustus seated on a dais, with Maecenas on his right. In front of the Emperor is Poetry which is personified by Homer, and three women who symbolize Painting, Sculpture and Architecture. The work is an allegory which alludes to the fact that Count Brühl, a minister at the Saxon Court, was a connoisseur of the arts, a collector of paintings, and adviser on questions of art to Augustus III, King of Poland and Elector of Saxony.
There is an engraving of the picture by Giacomo Leonardi.
The Magnanimity of Scipio in the National Museum in Stockholm is close in composition to the painting in the Hermitage.

The *Maecenas presenting the Liberal Arts to Augustus* was acquired in 1769 with the Brühl Collection; it was transferred to the Hermitage from the Gatchina Castle in 1882.

Literature:
Cat. 1912, p. 193, No 1671; Cat. 1958, I, p. 200, No 4; E. Sack, *Giambattista and Domenico Tiepolo*, Hamburg, 1910, p. 118, 206; P. Molmenti, *Giovanni Battista Tiepolo*, Milan, p. 282; S. N. Vsevolozhskaya, I. S. Grigoryeva, T. D. Fomicheva, *Italyanskaya zhivopis XIII–XVIII vekov v sobranii Ermitazha*, Leningrad, 1964, pp. 281, 303.

23   GIOVANNI BATTISTA TIEPOLO
       (1696–1770)

       MAECENAS PRESENTING THE LIBERAL ARTS
       TO THE EMPEROR AUGUSTUS
       (Detail)

24   ANTONIO CANALE (CANALETTO)
     (1697–1768)

THE RECEPTION OF THE FRENCH
AMBASSADOR AT VENICE
oil on canvas, 181 × 259.5 cm

This is a picture of the festival held in Venice on October 13th, 1726, in honour of the arrival of the French Ambassador, Count Gergi. The companion painting *The 'Bucentoro' leaving the Molo on Ascension Day* is now in the State Pushkin Museum of Fine Arts in Moscow.

There is no agreement as to the dating of these two works; some authorities date them to the 1740s, others to the 1730s. Two other pictures by Canaletto which are very close to the Hermitage painting, *The Reception of Count Bognolosa* and *The 'Bucentoro' preparing to leave the Molo on Ascension Day*, now in the collection of Aldo Crespi, Milan, are generally dated to Canaletto's early period.

Canaletto's spirited treatment of the Venetian crowd is closely observed, with the senators in their red mantles and white wigs, the oriental merchants, the monks, the urchins burning with curiosity, the gondoliers, and the masked figures. The sunlight and the sky with the vanishing clouds show the master's talents to their best advantage. The famous buildings in the centre of the city—the Doges' Palace, the Library, and the Church of Santa Maria della Salute—are executed with great topographical accuracy.

Acquired by the Hermitage between 1763 and 1774.

Literature:
Cat. 1912, p. 96, No 318; Cat. 1958, I, pp. 99, 102, No 175; W. Nisser, 'Lord Manchester's Reception at Venice', *The Burlington Magazine*, 1937 (January), p. 33; V. Moschini, *Canaletto*, 1954, pp. 18, 20, 62; W. G. Constable, *Canaletto, Giovanni Antonio Canale*, II, Oxford, 1962, pp. 345, 346, pl. 356.

25   ANTONIO CANALE (CANALETTO)
      (1697–1768)

      THE RECEPTION OF THE FRENCH
      AMBASSADOR AT VENICE
      (Detail)

26   ANTONIO CANALE (CANALETTO)
       (1697–1768)

**THE RECEPTION OF THE FRENCH
AMBASSADOR AT VENICE**
(Detail)

27 FRANCESCO GUARDI
(1702–1793)

LANDSCAPE
oil on canvas, 120×152 cm

Signed at bottom right: *Guardi*

The *Landscape* was most probably painted in the
1780s. The dark colouring of the picture, which is
painted in quick, vigorous strokes, is characteristic
of a number of Guardi's late works. The Hermitage
landscape is one of the few pictures by Guardi
where nature, and not architecture, forms the centre
of interest. In its romantic approach to nature the
Landscape is reminiscent of the paintings by Alessandro Magnasco.
The Hermitage painting is one of Guardi's masterpieces.

Transferred to the Hermitage in 1928 from the
Gatchina Castle.

Literature:
Cat. 1958, I, p. 82, No 4305; V. Lasareff, 'Francesco and Gianantonio Guardi', *The Burlington Magazine*, 1934 (August), p. 71; S. N. Vsevolozhskaya,
I. S. Grigoryeva, T. D. Fomicheva, *Italyanskaya
zhivopis XIII–XVIII vekov v sobranii Ermitazha*, Leningrad, 1964, pp. 287, 288, 304.

EL GRECO
(DOMENIKOS THEOTOKOPOULOS)
(1541–1614)

28

ST PETER AND ST PAUL

oil on canvas, 121.5 × 105 cm

This work, executed between 1587 and 1592, is one of the best of El Greco's paintings of St Peter and St Paul in his celebrated series of the *apostolados*. Taking as his starting point the few brief remarks in the Gospels, the Apocrypha and the Acts of the Apostles which reveal the characters of Christ's disciples, El Greco sought to individualize the personality of each apostle. St Paul is shown as an inspired preacher; St Peter, who deeply regretted his human weakness, is lost in his own sad thoughts. El Greco also characterizes the saints by the shape and gesture of their hands. The hands of the two apostles are in marked contrast. St Paul has aristocratic hands, pale and delicately shaped; St Peter's hands are rough and dark-skinned. St Paul seems to have just finished a vehement sermon—his lips are tightly closed, but his eyes are still burning with inner fire. To make the eyes more prominent against the pale face of the preacher, El Greco gave him a bare head and forehead. St Paul is passionate and impetuous, his cloak is painted with all the shades of red, from the deep, dark tone of old wine to scintillating pinks, so that it seems to be woven out of flames.

St Peter is treated entirely differently. His head is bent, his eyes are melancholy, his hair is grey and the left hand which holds the key hangs heavily as if drawn down by a great weight. St Peter is wearing a cloak of olive yellow, but reflections from St Paul's flaming cloak play on his garments too.

There are replicas of the Hermitage picture in the National Museum in Stockholm and in several private collections in Madrid and Barcelona, but they are inferior to the Hermitage painting both in depth of treatment and force of characterization. At the bottom right, below the signature, is the Greek word ΕΠΟΙΕ(Ι) which means 'made'. This has been misread as the date 1614 or 1618 in Cat. 1912 and in Cat. 1958, and also by P. Weiner, E. Liphart and T. Kaptereva.

Exhibited in the 1908 exhibition organized by the journal *Starye Gody*.

29 EL GRECO
(DOMENIKOS THEOTOCOPOLOS)
(1541–1614)

ST PETER AND ST PAUL
(Detail)

Presented to the Hermitage in 1911 by P. Durnovo.

Literature:
Cat. 1912, No 1962; Cat. 1958, I, p. 228, No 390;
E. Liphart, 'Ispanskiye khudozhniki XVI–XVII
veka', *Starye Gody*, 1908 (November), p. 719; J. von
Schmidt, 'Gemälde alter Meister im Petersburger
Privatbesitz', *Monatshefte für Kunstwissenschaft*, 1909,
II, p. 172; P. Weiner, 'Notizie di Russia. L'Espo-
sizione de quadri rivista "Starye Gody"', *L'Arte*,
Madrid, 1909, p. 227; Camon Aznar, *Domenico
Greco*, Madrid, 1950, p. 1377; T. P. Kaptereva,
Velasquez i ispansky portret XVII veka, Moscow, 1956,
p. 20; J. A. Gaya Nuño, *La pintura española fuera de
España. Historia y Catálogo*, Madrid, 1958, Cat. No
1271; I. M. Levina, *Ispanskoye iskusstvo XVI–XVII vv.*,
Moscow-Leningrad, 1965, pp. 91, 92.

JUAN PANTOJA DE LA CRUZ
(1553–1608)

PORTRAIT OF DIEGO DE VILLAMAYOR
oil on canvas, 89 × 71 cm

Signed and dated at bottom: *Jū Pantoja de la* ✠
Faciebat, 1605; the inscription above reads: *Didacus*
Villamaiori. Aetatis suae 17. Anno 1605.
In Cat. 1912 and Cat. 1958 the name of the sitter
is given incorrectly as Valmayor, and the date as
1609.

This is one of the most interesting portraits of Juan
Pantoja's late period. Following the iconography
of the official Spanish court portrait of the second
half of the sixteenth century, the master emphasized the details revealing the subject's rank. The
formal rigidity of his bearing, the serene expression, the majestic pose which denotes the proud
consciousness of the distance separating him from
ordinary mortals, are all typical features of the court
portrait. The badge of the Order of Alcántara hanging from the gold chain on the young man's breast
is carefully emphasized. The elegant linear ornament on the armour is painted with great attention
to detail; one well-groomed hand, with its narrow
palm and thin long fingers, rests on the hilt of the
sword and the other upon the helmet which is
placed on a stand by his side. The face is calm
and imperturbable. But more than the young man's
haughty aloofness is shown; his plain, ordinary
features are painted with great truthfulness, and
no attempt is made to idealize the sitter. This is
also typical of the Spanish portraiture of the period.

Acquired for the Hermitage in 1815 from the Coesvelt Collection, Amsterdam.

Literature:
Cat. 1912, No 1896; Cat. 1958, I, p. 242, No 3518;
T. P. Kaptereva, *Velasquez i ispansky portret XVII v.*,
Moscow, 1956, p. 17; L. L. Kagane, 'Daty i nad-
pisi na muzhskom portrete Juana Pantoji de
la Cruz', *Soobshcheniya Gosudarstvennogo Ermitazha*,
XXIV, Leningrad, 1963, pp. 21–25; I. M. Levina,
Ispanskoye iskusstvo XVI–XVII vv., Leningrad-
Moscow, 1965, pp. 75–76.

31 FRANCISCO RIBALTA
(1565–1628)

THE RAISING OF THE CROSS
oil on canvas, 144.5 × 103.5 cm

Signed and dated at the bottom right: *Franco Ribalta Catala lo pinto en Madrid Ano D. MDLXXXII*

This painting, which is the earliest known signed and dated canvas by Ribalta, was painted in 1582 in Madrid where he was studying the works of Venetian and Spanish masters. It shows the combined influences of S. del Piombo, Bassano and Juan Navarrete (El Mudo). The work is not yet as technically perfect as the artist's later pictures, but the realism of his mature period is already felt in the stern dramatic treatment, the choice of peasants as models, and the vivid characterization of the emotions. The picture may have formed part of a triptych.

Acquired for the Hermitage in 1815 from the Coesvelt Collection, Amsterdam.

Literature:
Cat. 1912, No 339; Cat. 1958, I, p. 245, No 303; D. Fitz Darby, *Francisco Ribalta and His School*, Cambridge, 1938, pp. 22, 71; T. P. Znamerovskaya, *Tvorchestvo Jusepe Ribery i problema narodnosti ispanskogo realisticheskogo iskusstva*, Leningrad, 1955, p. 53; J. A. Gaya Nuño, *La pintura española fuera de España. História y Catálogo*, Madrid, 1958, Hist. p. 58, Cat. No 2254.

JUAN BAUTISTA DEL MAYNO
(1578–1649)

ADORATION OF THE SHEPHERDS
oil on canvas, 142.5×101 cm

Signed on the fragment of column on the right:
F. IV B A

The *Adoration of the Shepherds* is one of the best
pictures by del Mayno. It is remarkable for the
brilliance of the colours and the effects of the con-
trasted tones of the blues, the reds and the yellows,
which are typical of this artist. The head of the old
man standing between the Madonna and the young
shepherd carrying a staff is reminiscent of El Greco,
with whom del Mayno studied for a time. The
figures in the group at the left, who are painted so
realistically, are portraits of the donors who are
thought to come from the court of King Philip IV.
The subject is taken from the New Testament
(Luke II, 8–17).

Acquired for the Hermitage in 1815 from the Coesvelt Collection, Amsterdam.

Literature:
Cat. 1912, No 414; Cat. 1958, I, p. 233, No 315;
A. L. Mayer, *Geschichte der spanischen Malerei*, Leipzig, 1922, p. 394; V. von Loga, *Die Malerei in
Spanien*, Berlin, 1923, p. 243; Lafuente Ferrari,
Breve historia de la pintura española, Madrid, 1953,
p. 231; J. A. Gaya Nuño, *La pintura española fuera
de España. Historia y Catálogo*, Madrid, 1958, Hist.
p. 56, Cat. No 1763.

33 PEDRO ORRENTE
(*c*. 1570–1645)

THE MIRACLE OF THE LOAVES AND FISHES
oil on canvas, 106 × 186 cm

The picture illustrates an episode from the New
Testament (Luke IX, 13–17). It is characteristic of
Orrente's treatment of Gospel subjects as genre
scenes. Many of the figures are inspired by the
work of the well-known Venetian artist Jacopo
Bassano—Orrente was called 'the Spanish Bassano' because of his enthusiastic admiration for the
Italian artist. The boy presenting a fish to Christ
and the seated woman in the right foreground are
particularly close to Bassano.
Orrente excelled in landscapes, in which he sur-
passed his teacher. The landscape in the Hermitage
picture is painted in a greenish tonality. The
winding roads, which are crowded with people,
run into the distance, skirting the rocks: this helps
to create the impression of a large crowd on the
march across a wide-open space. The red of the
basket-carriers' dresses can be seen in the distance
as they move away with their baskets full of loaves,
and further adds to the effect of distance.

Acquired for the Hermitage in 1815 from the Coesvelt Collection, Amsterdam.

Literature:
Cat. 1912, No 311a; Cat. 1958, I, p. 242, No 349;
A. L. Mayer, *Geschichte der spanischen Malerei*, Leipzig, 1922, p. 286; J. A. Gaya Nuño, *La pintura
española fuera de España. Historia y Catálogo*, Madrid,
1958, Hist. p. 260, Cat. No 2061; I. M. Levina,
Ispanskoye iskusstvo XVI–XVII vv., Moscow-Leningrad, 1965, p. 119.

JOSÉ RIBERA

34

(c. 1591–1652)

ST SEBASTIAN AND ST IRENE
oil on canvas, 156 × 188 cm

Signed and dated at bottom left: *Joseph A. Ribera Hisp. Valétin Se bê Acc. Rom. S. Partenope F. 1628*

The cult of St Sebastian, who was believed to be able to heal anyone suffering from the plague, was widespread in Catholic countries and his legend was extensively illustrated. In their pictures of St Sebastian, who was according to tradition a Roman captain executed at the command of the Emperor Diocletian for becoming a Christian, the masters of the Renaissance generally chose to paint a handsome youth who bore with courage the excruciating pain caused by the arrows which pierced his naked body. In the seventeenth century the theme of St Sebastian's heroic death was superseded by another episode of the legend which told how the rich widow Irene and her maid tried to succour the sufferer and ease his pain. The picture is one of Ribera's early works and is marked by a Caravaggesque influence in its dark, or *tenebroso*, manner. But it is far from Caravaggesque in the treatment of St Sebastian. Ribera created a profoundly tragic character of great spiritual beauty. St Sebastian is shown as a very thin and angular young man, almost a boy, about to die from his injuries. The entire composition focuses the attention of the viewer upon the gentle, lyrical and yet tragic beauty of St Sebastian. He lies on the ground, in the plane parallel to the canvas; one of his arms, with the wrist still tied to the stake, is raised, while the other has been freed and droops listlessly on the ground,

the fingers stiffened by the pain. The two women bending over his body are enveloped in shadow; and behind them is complete darkness. The foreground is filled with the body of the young martyr, which seems to throw off a golden light which irresistibly attracts the eye of the viewer. The saint's head is thrown back, his lips are half-parted and his nose is already sharpened to suggest that he is unconscious. Deep shadows suffuse the forehead, the bridge of the nose and the eyes, and show the final moment of the struggle between life and death.

Ribera returned to the subject of St Sebastian several times.

A version of the subject closely related to the Hermitage picture is in Valencia, Spain.

Acquired for the Hermitage in 1829 with the collection of the Duchesse de Saint Leu.

Literature:
Cat. 1912, No 331; Cat. 1958, I, p. 248, No 325; A. L. Mayer, *Jusepe de Ribera*, Leipzig, 1923, p. 62, 64; E. du Gué Trapier, *Ribera*, New York, 1952, pp. 43–46; Marc Sandoz, 'Ribera et le thème de "Saint Sebastien soigné par Irène"', *Cahiers de Bordeaux. Journées Internationales d'études d'art*, 1955, p. 86; T. P. Znamerovskaya, *Tvorchestvo Jusepe Ribery i problema narodnosti v ispanskom iskusstve*, Leningrad, 1955, pp. 78–81; J. A. Gaya Nuño, *La pintura española fuera de España*, Madrid, 1958, Cat. No 2273; I. M. Levina, *Ispanskoye iskusstvo XVI–XVII vekov*, Moscow-Leningrad, 1965, pp. 118–120.

35   JOSÉ RIBERA (?)
    (*c.* 1591–1652)

THE REPENTANCE OF ST PETER
oil on canvas, 75×63 cm

The subject, which was frequently illustrated in the seventeenth century, is taken from the New Testament (Luke XXII, 34–62).
Although a comparison of the figure of St Peter in this picture and in Ribera's etching of the same theme shows that they are close, and although the handling of the painting is close to that of Ribera's early period, there still remain some doubts as to the authenticity of this work. In particular, the handling of the colours seems unusual for a half-length figure of this type when compared with other authentic paintings by Ribera; and the canvas may have been painted by an artist of the Neapolitan school whose style was formed under Ribera's influence. This influence is felt in the rendering of the parted lips of the apostle, who seems to speak aloud his regret and repentance. The gnarled, toil-worn hands of the old man are most expressive.

Acquired by the Hermitage in 1923 from the collection of Prince K. A. Gorchakov, Petrograd.

Literature:
Cat. 1958, I, p. 248, No 4794; T. P. Znamerovskaya, *Tvorchestvo Jusepe Ribery i problema narodnosti v ispanskom realisticheskom iskusstve*, Leningrad, 1955, p. 210.

36 DIEGO VELASQUEZ
(1599–1660)

THE BREAKFAST
oil on canvas, 107×101 cm

The picture can be dated *c.* 1617–18, and is one of Velasquez's earliest genre scenes, which are called *bodegones* and which were executed at Seville in the studio of Pacheco. It belongs to a series of *bodegones* depicting a group of common people (generally two or three in all) at table. In this picture, as well as in the other early works by Velasquez, the strong contrasts of light and shade are used to organize the pictorial space. Skilful use is made of the light to highlight the faces, the white tablecloth with a cheap plate and a glass on it, and the plain food: a loaf of bread, several fishes, two pomegranates and some wine in a glass. The large figures of a youth, an old man and a boy are placed in the foreground and painted in half-length; this is characteristic of the *bodegones*. The figures are executed with a strong feeling for form: when they are in the light they stand out against the dark background, and when they are in the shadow they merge into it. On the dark wall in the background are several objects whose outlines can only just be made out; they are a collar, a cap and some weapons. The picture is executed in a simple, terse style; there is great reserve in the arrangement of the figures, in the choice of a few simple poses and gestures, and in the restricted range of the colours. Velasquez's superb mastery is displayed in the rendering of all the textures — the folds of the tablecloth, the crude thick faience of the plate, the handle of the knife and the ripe pomegranates with their thick skin and juicy pulp.

Closest to the Hermitage picture is a painting in Budapest. The old man in both pictures is painted from the same model. An interesting suggestion has been put forward by the Spanish scholar Cesar Pemán that the young man in yellow to the right of the Hermitage picture may be a self-portrait of the young Velasquez.

At one time the picture was in the Taurida Palace. It was acquired for the Hermitage before 1797 as a work by an unknown master of the Flemish school, and first attributed to Velasquez by A. Somov.

37 DIEGO VELASQUEZ
(1599–1660)

THE BREAKFAST
(Detail)

Literature:
Cat. 1912, No 1849; Cat. 1958, I, p. 224, No 389;
A. L. Mayer, *Velasquez. A Catalogue Raisonné of the Pictures and Drawings*, London, 1926, No XLIII; Lafuente Ferrari, *Velasquez*, London, 1943, No LXXIII; K. M. Malitskaya, *Ispanskaya zhivopis XVI–XVII vv.*, Moscow, 1947; I. M. Levina, *Diego Velasquez. Zavtrak*, Leningrad, 1948; T. P. Kaptereva, *Velasquez i ispansky portret XVII v.*, Moscow, 1956, p. 42; J. A. Gaya Nuño, *La pintura española fuera de España. Historia y Catálogo*, Madrid, 1958, Hist. p. 68, Cat. No 2810; T. P. Znamerovskaya, 'Sevilskie bodegones Velasqueza (k 300letiyu so dnya smerti)', *Vestnik Leningradskogo universiteta, No 2, seriya istorii, yazyka i literatury, vypusk I*, Leningrad, 1961, pp. 87–99; Cesar Pemán, 'Acerca de los llamados almuersos Velasqueños', *Archivo español de Arte*, 1961, No 136, pp. 303–311; *Velasquez A Catalogue Raisonné of his œuvre*, with an Introductory Study by José Lopez-Rey, London, 1963, pp. 26–28, Cat. No 113; I. M. Levina, *Ispanskoye iskusstvo XVI–XVII vv.*, Moscow-Leningrad, 1965, pp. 165–167.

38 DIEGO VELASQUEZ
(1599–1660)

THE BREAKFAST
(Detail)

39 DIEGO VELASQUEZ
(1599–1660)

PORTRAIT OF COUNT OLIVARES
oil on canvas, 67×45.5 cm

Don Gaspar de Guzman de Olivares, Duque de San Lúcar de Major (1587–1645), was minister to King Philip IV, and held his post from 1621 to 1643. A haughty, clever and masterful man, he exerted an almost unlimited influence over the monarch. His court career was ended in disgrace in 1643 by the successful intrigues of his numerous enemies.

His features, with the penetrating deep-set black eyes, the protruding lower lip and the shape of the eyebrows, only betray a stern, haughty temper and a self-centred, highly secretive and masterful personality. Velasquez succeeded in capturing the very essence of his subject's character — the vindictive cruelty combined with uncommon tenacity and resourcefulness — and created a portrait of striking artistic truthfulness. This distinguishes the Hermitage painting from the famous equestrian portrait of Olivares in the Prado. The composition is based on the contrasts of light and dark tones (the dark hair, eyes, moustache and dress are set against the white collar and the light flesh tone). The face, which is executed in a subtle colour scheme of redish and yellowish tons, is modelled with great mastery by the different shades of colours, with brush-strokes of varying length and shape to emphasize the form; this gives the portrait an almost tangible reality.

Velasquez painted several portraits of Olivares.

The age of the subject and the style of execution suggest a date about 1640. A number of replicas, probably by Velasquez's pupils, are known. Closest to the Hermitage painting is the portrait of Olivares now in Vienna.

Acquired for the Hermitage in 1815 from the Coesvelt Collection, Amsterdam.

Literature:
Cat. 1912, No 422; Cat. 1958, I, p. 224, No 300; A. Mayer, *Geschichte der spanischen Malerei*, Leipzig, 1922, p. 401; C. Justi, *Diego Velasquez und sein Jahrhundert*, Zürich, 1933, pp. 478–480; A. L. Mayer, *Velasquez. A Catalogue Raisonné of the Pictures and Drawings*, London, 1936, p. 77; M. V. Alpatoff. 'Ermitazhny "Olivares" Velasqueza', *Iskusstvo*, 1937, No 5, pp. 109–118; I. M. Levina, *Diego Velasquez. Portret Olivaresa*, Leningrad, 1948; T. P. Kaptereva, *Velasquez i ispansky portret XVII v.*, Moscow, 1956, pp. 66, 67; J. A. Gaya Nuño, *La pintura española fuera de España. Historia y Catálogo*, Madrid, 1958, Hist. p. 64, Cat. No 2852; *Velasquez. A Catalogue of his œuvre*, with an Introductory Study by José Lopez-Rey, London, 1963, p. 298, Cat. No 511; I. M. Levina, *Ispanskoye iskusstvo XVI–XVII vv.*, Moscow-Leningrad, 1965, pp. 186-187.

ANTONIO PUGA
(1602–1648)

THE KNIFE GRINDER
oil on canvas, 118 × 159 cm

The Hermitage canvas is probably one of the six genre scenes by A. Puga which were mentioned by Ceán Bermúdez. The theme often occurs in seventeenth-century European art, generally in drawings and engravings.
Puga's presentation of common people is marked by genuine sympathy and respect. His treatment is distinguished by its force and vitality. The artist's interest is centred on the group of figures; all details which might detract the attention from the figures are avoided—even the street is not shown. The knife grinder absorbed in his work, the young man handing him a coin, the soldier and the woman awaiting her turn are all invested with that dignified gravity which characterizes the treatment of common people in the works of Spanish masters. The young woman standing behind the soldier appears in another of Puga's pictures, his *Still-life with Figures*, now in the Castro Museum.

The picture was owned in the seventeenth century by Don Silvestro Collar y Castro, Secretary of the Council of the Indies. It was acquired for the Hermitage in 1815 from the Coesvelt Collection, Amsterdam.

Literature:
Cat. 1912, No 435; Cat. 1958, I, p. 245, No 309; J. A. Ceán Bermúdez, *Diccionario histórico de los illustres profesores de bellas artes en España*, IV, Madrid, 1800, p. 134; A. L. Mayer, *Geschichte der spanischen Malerei*, Leipzig, 1922, p. 42; L. Caturla, 'Un pintor gallego en la corte de Philipe IV, Antonio Puga', *Cuadernos de estudios gallegos*, No 6, 1952, p. 10; J. A. Gaya Nuño, *La pintura española fuera de España. Historia y Catálogo*, Madrid, 1958, Hist. p. 67, Cat. No 2223; I. M. Levina, *Ispanskoye iskusstvo XVI–XVII vv.*, Moscow-Leningrad, 1965, p. 220.

41 FRANCISCO DE ZURBARÁN
(c. 1598–1664)

ST LAWRENCE
oil on canvas, 292 × 225 cm

Signed and dated at the right on the gridiron:
Fdezurbaran facie 1636

This is one of the master's best pictures and the
composition with a single figure in the foreground
is very characteristic of Zurbarán. The saint is
shown with his attribute, a gridiron. According to
the legend St Lawrence, one of the seven deacons
of Rome and a disciple of Pope Sixtus II, was
martyred by being roasted to death on a gridiron
in 258, during the reign of the Emperor Valerian.
The subject was common in European art both
in easel paintings and in mosaics and frescoes;
different episodes of the legend were chosen for
illustration. Zurbarán chose to represent St Lawrence going to his death. The saint is a big, strong,
yet austere man. He is deeply agitated, his gaze is
directed towards the sky, his lips are parted, a
shadow lurks in the bitter lines at the sides of his
mouth, but the gesture of his right hand is simple
and restrained. The figure has a monumental
quality: the lower part of the white vestment, with
its heavy folds, suggests a pedestal; the pomegranate-
red sticharion, ornamented with raised gold embroidery, is painted with an extraordinarily vivid
sense of texture. The figure is set against a broad
expanse of clear sky which stretches above a mountain valley. Warm golden tones provide the background for the martyr's head; lower they merge
with silvery greys. For the *St Lawrence* Zurbarán
probably used as his model a monk of the Order

of Discalced Mercedarians whose portrait, which
was painted by Zurbarán in 1628, is now in the
collection of Maria Cruzat de Romeo de Armaz,
Madrid.
The nearest parallels for the *St Lawrence* are provided by two large pictures in the Seville Museum
showing respectively *St Enrique Suso* and *St Louis
Bertram;* the figures are painted full length, against
a landscape background.
The *St Lawrence* was painted for the transept of the
Mercedarian Church in Seville.

In 1810 the picture was in the Alcázar, Seville. It
was taken away by Soult, one of Napoleon's mar-
shals, and acquired for the Hermitage in 1852 at
the sale of Soult's pictures.

Literature:
Cat. 1912, No 349; Cat. 1958, I, p. 250, No 361;
A. Ponz, *Viage de España*, IX, Madrid, 1712, p. 350;
Ceán Bermúdez, *Diccionario histórico de los ilustres
profesores de las bellas artes en España*, I, Madrid,
1800, pp. 44–52; M. S. Soria, *The Paintings of Zur-
barán*, London, 1955, pp. 160–161, No 117; J. A.
Gaya Nuño, *La pintura española fuera de España.
Historia y Catálogo*, Madrid, 1958, Hist. p. 62, Cat.
No 3030; P. Guinard, *Zurbarán et les peintres es-
pagñols de la vie monastique*, Paris, 1960, pp, 147, 234,
Cat. No 225; I. M. Levina, 'Sv. Lavrenty i yego
proobraz', *Soobshcheniya Gosudarstvennogo Ermitazha*,
XX, 1961, pp. 20–23; K. M. Malitskaya, *Zurbarán*,
Moscow, 1963, p. 73; I. M. Levina, *Ispanskoye
iskusstvo XVI–XVII vv.*, Moscow-Leningrad, 1965,
pp. 155–159.

FRANCISCO DE ZURBARÁN
(*c.* 1598–1664)

THE VIRGIN MARY AS A CHILD
oil on canvas, 73.5×53.5 cm

Both the style and subject of this work, painted *c.* 1660, are characteristic of the late period of Zurbarán's career, when his religious pictures became more lyrical. The girl in the Hermitage painting is a triumphant example of the master's art. She may have been the artist's daughter. Zurbarán's treatment of the subject is marked by unaffected simplicity, sincerity and great lyrical charm. The child's face is raised towards the sky with a look of gentle confidence and her hands are folded in her lap. The pose of the girl expresses her meekness and modesty; this is further emphasized by the simplicity of her dress, which is unadorned except for a single narrow band of embroidery. There is a refined and careful choice of colours (reds, blues, whites and greens) which form subtly contrasting combinations.

Several versions of the subject are known. Closest to the Hermitage painting is the picture in the collection of M. Gomez Moreno, Madrid, also datable *c.* 1660. P. Guinard suggests an earlier date for the Hermitage painting, namely *c.* 1650.

Acquired for the Hermitage in 1815 from the Coesvelt Collection, Amsterdam.

Literature:
Cat. 1912, No 348; Cat. 1958, I, p. 250, No 306; M. S. Soria, *The Paintings of Zurbarán*, London, 1955, pp. 20, 22, No 211; T. P. Kaptereva, *Velasquez i ispansky portret XVII v.*, Moscow, 1956, p. 37; J. Y. Gaya Nuño, *La pintura española fuera de España. Historia y Catálogo*, Madrid, 1958, Hist. p. 71, Cat. No 3130; P. Guinard, *Zurbarán et les peintres espagnols de la vie monastique*, Paris, 1960, p. 27; K. M. Malitskaya, *Zurbarán*, Moscow, 1963, p. 84; I. M. Levina, *Ispanskoye iskusstvo XVI–XVII vv.*, Moscow-Leningrad, 1965, p. 162.

43 BARTOLOMÉ ESTEBAN MURILLO
(1617–1682)

ISAAC BLESSING JACOB
oil on canvas, 246 × 357.5 cm

This painting, which was executed between 1660 and 1670, is one of the best in the Hermitage collection of Murillos. The landscape, which shows an infinite variety of tones, from heavy dark greys, the colour of smoke, to light transparent silvery ones, and which is enlivened here and there by touches of pink and gold, is executed by a true virtuoso. The birds flying away into the distance, the narrow path disappearing beyond the rocks, the woman hurrying along the path, her body slightly bent under the weight of the jar of water, and the wall of the house seen in perspective, perpendicular to the surface of the picture, all serve to create an illusion of depth, and lead the gaze of the viewer towards the mountains in the distance. The light is diffused; dark and golden shadows race along the ground. The pink of the walking woman's skirt relieves the gloom of the grey tones; it harmonizes with the dark mass of the well and is echoed by the gleam of subdued gold on the brass basin by the wall. The story, which is taken from the Bible (Genesis XXVII, 18–29), is only of secondary importance. The more interesting of the two figures at the old man's bedside is Rebecca, who is shown as an elderly woman, thin and worn, and full of worry—a favourite type with Murillo. This type will also be found in the *Adoration of the Shepherds* (Prado), *The Education of the Virgin* (Prado), *The Holy Family*, and other pictures by the master.

This is one of the pictures from the Jacob cycle. In the seventeenth century the whole series, which had been executed for the Marquis de Villamanrique, Protector of the Academy of Arts in Seville, was in his collection; in the eighteenth century the pictures were owned by the Marquis de Santiago, and were in his palace in Madrid. The Hermitage picture was taken from Spain to France by Sébastiani, one of Napoleon's generals, as part of the contribution paid to the French by the city of Madrid. It was acquired for the Hermitage in 1811, through the agency of Baron Vivant Denon, together with *The Vision of Jacob*, another work from the same cycle.

Literature:
Cat. 1912, No 360; Cat. 1958, I, p. 236, No 332; C. Justi, *Murillo*, Leipzig, 1904; A. L. Mayer, *Murillo. Klassiker der Kunst*, Stuttgart-Berlin, 1913, p. 19; A. L. Mayer, *Geschichte der spanischen Malerei*, Leipzig, 1922, p. 34; D. A. Schmidt, *Murillo*, Leningrad, 1926, p. 10; K. M. Malitskaya, *Ispanskaya zhivopis XVI–XVII vv.*, Moscow, 1947, p. 81; G. Rouchés, *La peinture espagnole*, Paris, 1958, p. 255; J. A. Gaya Nuño, *La pintura española fuera de España. Historia y Catálogo*, Madrid, 1958, Hist. p. 69, Cat. No 1943; I. M. Levina, 'Narodnye obrazy v proizvedeniakh Murillo', *Iskusstvo*, 1959, No 5, p. 65; I. M. Levina, *Ispanskoye iskusstvo XVI–XVII vv.*, Moscow-Leningrad, 1965, pp. 240–242.

44   BARTOLOMÉ ESTEBAN MURILLO
(1617–1682)

ISAAC BLESSING JACOB
(Detail)

45 BARTOLOMÉ ESTEBAN MURILLO
(1617–1682)

BOY WITH A DOG
oil on canvas, 77.5×61.5 cm

This painting, which can be dated to 1650s, is one of the earliest genre scenes by Murillo, who painted the poor children of Seville throughout the whole of his career.

This picture, like *The Beggar Boy* (Louvre) and some others, is still free from that preference for pretty children which can be seen in *The Dice Players* (Munich) or *The Good Shepherd* (Prado) and which is such a marked feature in Murillo's work of the late period.

The charm of the boy in the Hermitage picture owes little to good looks, it lies in the open-heartedness and sincerity of childhood. The friendly smile which lights his face as he looks at the dog and the gesture with which he shows his four-footed friend that his basket is empty are both natural and expressive.

The boy in the Hermitage picture was probably painted from the same model as the boy in the *Peasant Boy leaning on a Sill* in the National Gallery, London.

The companion to the *Boy with a Dog, The Orange-Seller*, is now in the State Pushkin Museum of Fine Arts in Moscow.

Acquired for the Hermitage in 1772 at the sale of the collection of the Duc de Choiseul, Paris.

Literature:
Cat. 1912, No 348; Cat. 1958, I, p. 250, No 306; A. L. Mayer, *Murillo. Klassiker der Kunst*, Stuttgart-Berlin, 1913, p. 207; A. L. Mayer, *Geschichte der spanischen Malerei*, Leipzig, 1922, p. 342; D. A. Schmidt, *Murillo*, Leningrad, 1926, p. 6; J. A. Gaya Nuño, *La pintura española fuera de España. Historia y Catálogo*, Madrid, 1958, Hist. p. 68, Cat. No 1870; I. M. Levina, 'Narodnye obrazy v proizvedeniyakh Murillo', *Iskusstvo*, 1959, No 5, p. 69; I. M. Levina, *Ispanskoye iskusstvo XVI–XVII vv.*, Moscow-Leningrad, 1965, pp. 251, 252.

46 BARTOLOMÉ ESTEBAN MURILLO
(1617–1682)

BOY WITH A DOG
(Detail)

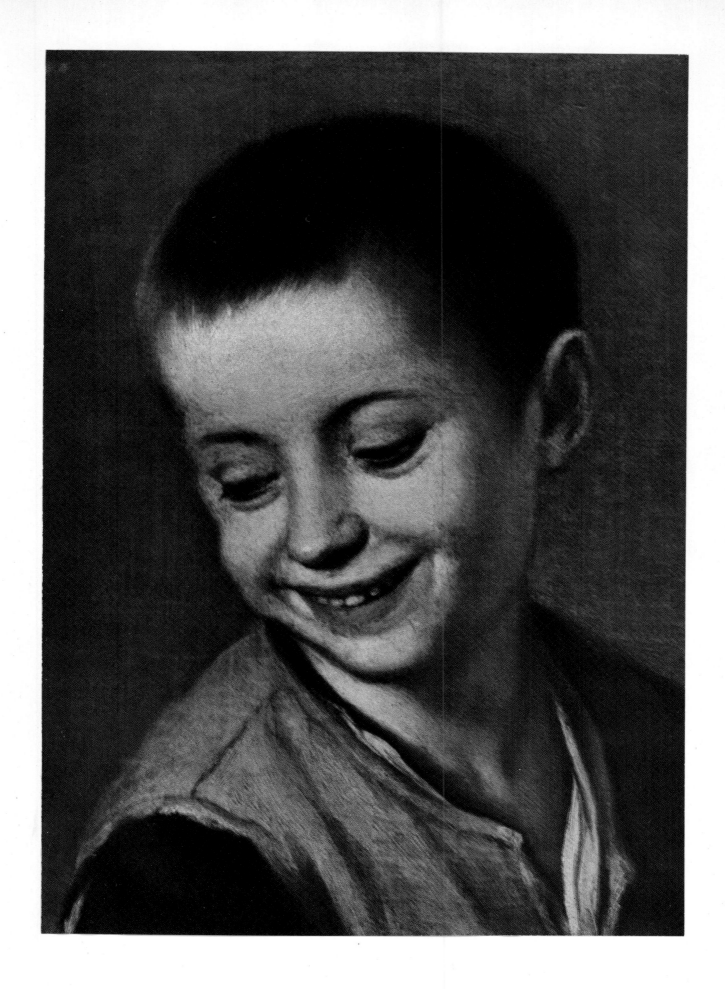

47 BARTOLOMÉ ESTEBAN MURILLO
(1617–1682)

REST ON THE FLIGHT INTO EGYPT
oil on canvas, 138.5 × 180 cm

In the refinement of its colouring, the harmony of the composition and the beauty of the figures this painting ranks high among Murillo's masterpieces. It dates from the artist's mature period, between 1665 and 1670. A sense of rest and peace pervades the quiet summer evening. The infant Christ sleeps on a stone at the roadside and the bundles containing the scanty belongings of the travellers, which were hurriedly packed at their departure, are laid near by. The painting shows great mastery, and an excellent feeling for textures. Joseph, who stands in the shadow of the branches, bends down to the Child. The two putti look at the sleeping baby with frank, childish curiosity.

The Madonna and Child form the centre of the composition. The Madonna has that fragile and graceful type of beauty which is favoured by Murillo, and which he found in the young girls of Andalusia. Her gaze is directed downwards and she shields the Child with a protective gesture of her open left hand.

The figures are arranged in a diagonal, and Joseph's head on the right of the picture forms its highest point. The diagonals are carried down smoothly and gradually to reach the putti, and are repeated in the outlines of the trees and hills. The colour scheme is also full of subtle harmony: the light red of the Madonna's garments, the brownish tone of Joseph's clothes, the dark trees, the golden hues in the bodies of the putti and the bluish tints of their little wings which harmonize with the smoky grey of the distant mountains.

The picture was painted for the convent of Mercedarians in Seville.

Acquired for the Hermitage in 1768 at the sale of the collection of Gaignat, former secretary to Louis XV, through the agency of Denis Diderot.

Literature:
Cat. 1912, No 367; Cat. 1958, I, p. 237, No 370; A. L. Mayer, *Murillo. Klassiker der Kunst*, Stuttgart-Berlin, 1913, p. 51; D. A. Schmidt, *Murillo*, Leningrad, 1926, pp. 15, 16; J. A. Gaya Nuño, *La pintura española fuera de España. Historia y Catálogo*, Madrid, 1958, Cat. No 1900; I. M. Levina, 'Narodnye obrazy v proizvedeniyakh Murillo', *Iskusstvo*, 1959, No 5, p. 64; I. M. Levina, *Ispanskoye iskusstvo XVI–XVII vv.*, Moscow-Leningrad, 1965, pp. 239, 240.

48   BARTOLOMÉ ESTEBAN MURILLO
(1617–1682)

REST ON THE FLIGHT INTO EGYPT
(Detail)

49 ANTONIO PEREDA
(*c.* 1608–1678)

STILL-LIFE
oil on canvas, 80×94 cm

Signed in the centre, on one of the boxes: *Pereda f.*

The still-life shows a group of objects which are
executed with great mastery; but it represents a
change from the austere simplicity of Zurbarán's
still-lifes, and Velasquez's *bodegones.* A gay, even
gaudy, note appears in the colouring. The many
objects are grouped close together. An obvious
desire for a decorative effect can be seen in the
introduction of the figured fabric falling from the
box, which harmonizes with the scarlet tablecloth
and the red vases. But the still-life is not a haphazard arrangement of unrelated objects, in contrast
with Pereda's later pictures *The Dream of the Knight,*
in the San Fernando Academy of Fine Arts, Madrid,
or the *Vanitas* in the Kunsthistorisches Museum,
Vienna, in which the objects are meant to serve
as reminders of the vanity of life.
The companion to the Hermitage painting, the
Still-life with a Clock and Shells, is now in the State
Pushkin Museum of Fine Arts in Moscow.

Acquired for the Hermitage in 1815 from the Coesvelt Collection, Amsterdam.

Literature:
Cat. 1912, No 416; Cat. 1958, I, p. 245, No 327;
A. L. Mayer, *Geschichte der spanischen Malerei,* Leip-
zig, 1922, p. 435; K. M. Malitskaya, *Ispanskaya
zhivopis XVI–XVII vv.,* Moscow, 1947, p. 163; P.
Guinard and J. Baticle, *Histoire de la peinture
espagnole,* Paris, 1950, p. 169; J. A. Gaya Nuño, *La
pintura española fuera de España. Historia y Catálogo,*
Madrid, 1958, Hist. p. 71, Cat. No 2179; I. M.
Levina, *Ispanskoye iskusstvo XVI–XVII vv.,* Moscow-
Leningrad, 1965, pp. 220, 221.

LOUIS LE NAIN
(*c.* 1593–1648)

THE MILKMAID'S FAMILY
oil on canvas, 51 × 59 cm

This is one of the best paintings by Louis Le Nain, who took his subjects from the life of the French peasantry. The appeal of this simple everyday scene lies in the directness and sincerity of the treatment and the superb execution. An elderly woman with a brass milk-can slung over her shoulder, a man, a boy and a girl form a group around the small saddled donkey. The artist placed the figures on a strip of high ground behind which there is a wide stretch of low plain. This gives the picture, in spite of its modest size, a certain monumental quality. The simple peasants are grave and dignified, and the whole scene loses its prosaic quality and takes on a deeper meaning.

The Milkmaid's Family was painted during the artist's best period, in the 1640s, when he was particularly interested in landscape painting. But Louis Le Nain never painted landscape for its own sake. The lonely plain of Normandy, which is so faithfully rendered in this picture, serves as a setting for the figures. And yet Le Nain's landscapes, which are bathed in light and air, anticipate the plein-air scenes of nineteenth-century masters. The dominating silvery tone gives unity to the colouring. The

delicate effects of light flooding through the picture give it a deeply poetic quality. The simple implements belonging to the peasants grouped in the foreground—a wooden tub, a bucket and a pole—are enveloped in a shadow so soft and translucent that it suggests the vibration of the surrounding air. Le Nain had the gift of seeing beauty in everyday life and in commonplace objects which, like Chardin after him, he transformed by the magic of his art into great paintings.

Acquired for the Hermitage between 1774 and 1783.

Literature:
Cat. 1903, No 1493 (The Brothers Le Nain; the name is not specified); Cat. 1958, I, p. 391, No 1152; P. Fierens, *Les frères Le Nain*, Cat. No 24; G. Isarlov, 'Les trois Le Nain', *La Renaissance*, 1938, III, Cat. No 245; V. Lasareff, *Bratya Le Nain*, Moscow, 1938, pp. 48, 50–52; V. Bloch. 'Louis Le Nain and his brothers', *The Burlington Magazine*, 1939 (March), pp. 53, 54; Ch. Sterling, *Musée de l'Ermitage. La peinture française*, Paris, 1957, p. 19.

51 LOUIS LE NAIN
(c. 1593–1648)

THE MILKMAID'S FAMILY
(Detail)

LOUIS LE NAIN
(*c.* 1593–1648)

A VISIT TO GRANDMOTHER
oil on canvas, 58 × 73 cm

The picture is a typical Le Nain, showing the specific French peasant genre in which the master specialized. The somewhat coarse, good-natured story-telling of the peasant scenes by his Dutch and Flemish contemporaries is completely alien to the austere simplicity of Le Nain's art. A certain rigidity in the attitudes and a tendency towards sketchy generalization in the handling of forms are the essential ingredients of Le Nain's style, and serve to create a mood of profound tranquillity and repose and to invest the characters with a grave dignity.

The composition of the unpretentious family group with an old grandmother among her grandchildren suggests an antique bas-relief. A slight gesture and a hardly perceptible movement of the body are cleverly used to knit the figures into a group and to underline the emotional ties which link together the characters. The pretty boys singing to the accompaniment of a reed-pipe for their grandmother's amusement lend a subtle poetic charm to the picture.

Painted between 1640 and 1648.

Acquired in 1772 with the Crozat Collection, Paris.

Literature:
Cat. 1903, No 1493; Cat. 1958, I, p. 301, No 1172; P. Jamot, *Petit Palais*, 1934, Cat. No 18; G. Isarlov; 'Les trois Le Nain', *La Renaissance*, 1938, III, Cat. No 255; P. Fierens, *Les frères Le Nain*, Cat. No 25; V. Lasareff, *Bratya Le Nain*, Moscow, 1938, pp. 41–48; V. Bloch, 'Louis Le Nain and his brothers', *The Burlington Magazine*, 1939 (March), pp. 53, 54; Ch. Sterling, *Musée de l'Ermitage. La peinture française*, Paris, 1957, p. 18.

53 JEAN DARET
(1615–1668)

SELF-PORTRAIT
oil on canvas, 78 × 66 cm

Signed and dated at bottom left: *Daret J. fecit 1636
aetatis suae 21*

The picture is of great interest as one of the few
surviving works by a provincial seventeenth-
century artist whose *œuvre* has not yet been properly
investigated. Daret was a Fleming by birth: in his
youth he visited Italy, where he studied mainly the
work of Guercino and Guido Reni. In 1639 he
settled at Aix, in the south of France, and lived
there until his death in 1668.
The inscription, giving the artist's age in 1636,
made it possible to establish the date of his birth
which previously had been erroneously given as
1613.

Formerly in the Myatlev Collection, Petrograd,
since 1923 in the Hermitage.

Literature:
Cat. 1958, I, p. 283, No 5704; A. Benois, 'Sobraniye
M. Myatlevoy v Peterburge', *Zolotoye Runo*, 1906,
Nos 11, 12, p. 38; A. Benois, *Istoriya zhivopisi*, IV,
Petrograd, p. 140; S. Ernst, 'Exposition de la pein-
ture française des XVII–XVIIIe s. au Musée de
l'Ermitage', *Gazette des Beaux-Arts*, 1928, p. 165;
Ch. Sterling, *Musée de l'Ermitage. La peinture fran-
çaise*, Paris, 1957, pp. 24, 215, No 39.

NICOLAS POUSSIN
(1593–1665)

54

TANCRED AND ERMINIA
oil on canvas, 98.5 × 146.5 cm

The picture illustrates an episode from *Jerusalem Liberated*, by Torquato Tasso, the sixteenth-century Italian poet (Canto XIX). Erminia, Princess of Antioch, finds her beloved Tancred, a Crusader knight, lying wounded on the field of battle. She cuts off a strand of her hair with which to bandage his wounds.

The painting is datable to the period 1630 to 1635, when Poussin began to paint his first masterpieces. Poussin was inspired by an ideal of beauty and grandeur, which he derived from his studies of classic art and of the art of Raphael, but at the same time he deeply appreciated the charm of Titian's rich palette. It was Titian who revealed to him the great emotional value of colour. The Hermitage picture, which is painted in broad free strokes on coarse-weave canvas, shows Poussin's mastery of forceful, expressive colouring. The stormy sunset sky, tinged with scarlet, suffuses the picture with reflections of pale gold. The strawberry red of Tancred's garments, the luminous yellow of the servant's dress and the blues in Erminia's tunic—from the soft, lyrical pale tint to the sombre, tragic tone the deepest hue—all echo the colours in the sunset sky. As accompaniment is subsidiary to melody, so is the landscape to the figures; its functions are to intensify the colour effects and to enhance the prevailing mood. The composition has the order and clarity so typical of Poussin's style and this helps the viewer to grasp the main points of the story. The composition directs the eye to the protagonists and links the figures in a common movement. The silvery sheen of the armour and the delicate play of yellow, red and blue reflections on it are executed in a masterly fashion.

Another picture illustrating a subject taken from Tasso's poem, the *Rinaldo and Armida*, is now at the State Pushkin Museum of Fine Arts in Moscow. The Barber Institute of the University of Birmingham owns a version of *Tancred and Erminia* related to the Hermitage painting. Some authorities (Bodkin, Blunt, Sterling) maintain that it is later than our version. In our opinion, however, it is earlier than the Hermitage canvas: the crowded composition, the size of the figures, the deliberately emphatic gestures and attitudes all link the Barber version with the group of pictures painted around 1630 (*The Vision of St Jacob*, Louvre; *Rinaldo and Armida*, Dulwich). But the desire to achieve the most logical and clear composition and the depth of poetic feeling in the Hermitage *Erminia* make it close to *The Realm of Flora* (Dresden), which is dated to the middle 'thirties of the seventeenth century.

Exhibited at the 1937 Exhibition of Masterpieces of French Painting in the National Fine Arts Museum (Paris, 1937, No 112) and at the Exhibition of the Works of Poussin in the Louvre (1960, No 42).

55 NICOLAS POUSSIN
(1593–1665)

TANCRED AND ERMINIA
(Detail)

Acquired for the Hermitage at the sale of the painter Aved's collection, Paris, 1766.

Literature:
Cat. 1903, No 1408; Cat. 1958, I, p. 326, No 1189; *Exposition Nicolas Poussin*, the Louvre, Paris, 1960, Cat. No 42; O. Grautoff, *Nicolas Poussin*, II, Berlin, 1914, Cat. No 39; E. Magne, *Nicolas Poussin*, Paris, 1914, Cat. No 339; V. N. Volskaya, *Nicolas Poussin*, Moscow, 1936; Ch. Sterling, *Musée de l'Ermitage. La peinture française*, Paris, 1957, pp. 20, 30; D. Mahon, 'Poussin's Early Development', *The Burlington Magazine*, 1960 (July), pp. 298, 299; M. Alpatoff, 'Poussin, peintre d'histoire', *Colloque international*, 1960, I, pp. 192, 193; A. S. Glikman, *Nicolas Poussin*, Leningrad-Moscow, 1964, pp. 43, 44.

56 NICOLAS POUSSIN
(1593–1665)

MOSES STRIKING THE ROCK
oil on canvas, 122.5 × 193 cm

The subject of the picture is taken from the Bible (Exodus XVII). Moses saves the people of Israel from death by thirst during their wanderings in the wilderness on their long and difficult journey to the Promised Land.

According to Félibien and Bellori, who give an accurate description of the picture, it was executed in 1649 for the painter Jacques Stella. An earlier version (1635–1636), which is close to the Hermitage painting, is in the collection of Lord Ellesmere, in London. There is another version, now in the Louvre, from the Pearson Collection. Two other versions are known from engravings executed by Soyer and E. Lingée.

There are two drawings for the picture in the Hermitage collection and one in the Louvre.

An engraving of the picture was made in 1687 by Cl. Bouzonnet-Stella.

Moses striking the Rock is one of the works in which Poussin treated the whole crowd, and not any individual or group of individuals, as the protagonist. The composition is so arranged that the figures, which are linked by their gestures, merge into a single crowd animated by a common spirit.

The picture changed hands several times. In the seventeenth and eighteenth centuries it was in the collection of Jacques Stella, later in the collections of C. Bouzonnet-Stella, of M. A. Molandier and, lastly, of Walpole who acquired it around 1733. It was acquired for the Hermitage in 1779 with the Walpole Collection.

Exhibited at the 1960 Exhibition of Poussin's Works in the Louvre (No 88).

Literature:
Cat. 1903, No 1394; Cat. 1958, I, p. 331, No 1177; Exposition Nicolas Poussin, the Louvre, Paris, 1960, No 88; G. P. Bellori, *Vite de' Pittori, Sculptori, etc.,* Rome, 1678 (ed. Piza, 1826, VII, p. 158); Félibien, *Entretiens sur les ouvrages des plus fameux peintres,* IV, Paris, 1725, p. 60; *Aedes Walpolianae,* p. 92; E. Magne, *Nicolas Poussin,* Paris, 1914, No 149; O. Grautoff, *Nicolas Poussin,* 1914, p. 91; W. Weisbach, *Französische Malerei,* 1914, p. 92; V. N. Volskaya, *Nicolas Poussin,* Moscow, 1936; V. K. Guertz, 'Kartina Poussina, Moïsey Issekayushchy vodu iz skaly', *Trudy Gosudarstvennogo Ermitazha,* 1941, pp. 150–164; T. Bertin-Mourot, 'Moïse frappant le rocher', *Société Poussin. Premier Cahier,* 1947 (June), p. 61; Ch. Sterling, *Musée de l'Ermitage. La peinture française,* Paris, 1957, p. 31; J. Tuillier, *Colloque international Nicolas Poussin,* I, pp. 128, 214; Francastel, *Colloque international Nicolas Poussin,* I, Paris, p. 206; A. S. Glikman, *Nicolas Poussin,* Leningrad-Moscow, 1964, pp. 69–72.

NICOLAS POUSSIN
(1593–1665)

LANDSCAPE WITH POLYPHEMUS
oil on canvas, 150 × 198 cm

The subject is taken from Ovid's *Metamorphoses* (Book XIII, 760–856). The one-eyed giant Polyphemus, the violence of whose temper used to make everybody fly from him in horror, falls victim to the charms of the fair nymph Galatea, and plays love songs in her honour on huge pipes.

The companion to this painting, *Landscape with Hercules and Cacus*, is now at the State Pushkin Museum of Fine Arts in Moscow.

Félibien, a contemporary of the artist, says that the landscape was painted in 1649 at the order of the banker Pointel, an enlightened patron of the arts and a friend of Poussin. But a study of the brushwork points to a later date in the 1650s. It is not improbable that the pictures may have been ordered by Pointel in 1649 when on a visit to Rome, and executed later (the Moscow landscape may even be as late as the beginning of the 1660s). During the earlier period of Poussin's career he had treated landscape merely as a setting for his compositions with many figures. From the middle of the 1640s, however, his interest in landscape quickened and he began to paint pure landscapes. He used landscapes to illustrate his philosophy and to glorify the creative power of nature as the embodiment of Universal Reason.

Landscape with Polyphemus is an outstanding Poussin. It expresses his worship of the might and beauty of nature which are the source of all inspiration, and of all thought and emotion, in man. The awful Polyphemus, whose body seems to be the summit of a rock, is conquered by the power of love, and is a poetic metaphor which suggests the final victory of the forces of light and harmony over the unbridled elemental forces both in man and nature. There is a small replica (49 × 66 cm) in the Prado, Madrid (Cat. 1942, No 2392, which some specialists consider to be a sketch in oils for this picture).

58 NICOLAS POUSSIN
(1593–1665)

LANDSCAPE WITH POLYPHEMUS
(Detail)

Acquired for the Hermitage in 1772 from the collection of Marquis de Conflans through the agency of Diderot.
Exhibited at the 1960 Exhibition of Poussin's Works in the Louvre (No 89).

Literature:
Cat. 1903, No 1414; Cat. 1958, I, p. 331, No 1186; Nicolas Poussin Exhibition, the Louvre, Paris, 1960, No 89; Félibien, *Entretiens sur les ouvrages des plus fameux peintres*, IV, Paris, 1725, p. 59; W. Friedländer, *Nicolas Poussin*, Munich, 1914; E. Magne, *Nicolas Poussin*, Paris, 1914, Cat. No 307, p. 217; O. Grautoff, *Nicolas Poussin*, II, Berlin, 1914, Cat. No 135, p. 210; W. Weisbach, *Die französische Malerei*, Berlin, 1932, p. 318, 369; V. N. Volskaya, *Nicolas Poussin*, Moscow, 1936, pp. 128–131; V. K. Guertz, *Landscape with Polyphemus*, Leningrad, 1960; A. S. Glikman, *Nicolas Poussin*, Leningrad-Moscow, 1964, pp. 81–83.

59 CLAUDE LORRAIN (CLAUDE GELLÉE)
(1600–1682)

MORNING IN THE HARBOUR
oil on canvas, 97.5 × 120.5 cm

Lorrain was one of the first French painters to convey in his canvases the magic of light and air, and to capture the varying effects of light at different times of day. Pictures of seaports with fantastic palaces rising along the coast play an important part in his *œuvre*. The sea in all its manifold aspects had a strong appeal for his imagination: the reflection of the sky in its surface at sunrise, the varying, shifting lights and the gleam and glitter of the waves were effects which he loved to paint. The disc of the rising sun in our picture is painted with a boldness which is unusual for Lorrain's time, and the rendering of light and air anticipates the approach of Turner and the Impressionists. Lorrain's works enjoyed immense popularity, and there were frequent attempts to produce forgeries. To check this, Lorrain executed drawings after a great number of his paintings. The resultant book, containing 200 of these drawings, was called the *Liber Veritatis* by Lorrain himself. On the verso of many of the drawings is the date and the name of the patron for whom the work was executed (the *Liber Veritatis* is now in the British Museum in London). The *Morning in the Harbour* was painted *c.* 1649 for Philibert-Emmanuel de Laverdan, Archbishop of Mans. The composition may be traced to an etching done by Lorrain in 1636. A replica made in 1674 is in the Munich Pinakothek (Cat. 1918, No 1327). The *Liber Veritatis* drawing No 5.

Acquired for the Hermitage in 1779 with the Walpole Collection from Houghton Hall, Norfolk, England.

Literature:
Cat. 1903, No 1437 (*Evening in the Harbour*); Cat. 1958, I, p. 305, No 1243 (*Morning in the Harbour*); *Aedes Walpolianae*, p. 137; M. Patisson, *Claude Lorrain, sa vie, etc.*, Paris, 1884, pp. 208, 246; W. Friedländer, *Claude Lorrain*, Berlin, 1926, pp. 106, 239, 242; M. Rothlisberger, *Claude Lorrain*, I, 1961, p. 103.

60   CLAUDE LORRAIN (CLAUDE GELLÉE)
      (1600–1682)

      MORNING IN THE HARBOUR
      (Detail)

CLAUDE LORRAIN (CLAUDE GELLÉE)
(1600–1682)

REST ON THE FLIGHT INTO EGYPT (NOON)
oil on canvas, 113 × 157 cm

Signed with a hardly legible inscription and dated
at bottom right: *Claudi Rue Ro 1651* (?)

The picture forms part of the famous series *The
Four Times of Day (Morning, Noon, Evening, Night)*.
The paintings were executed at different times and
for different patrons, and the idea of treating them
as a set was only conceived in the eighteenth
century. The only picture of the series which originally had a pendant is *Noon;* the companion
picture, *Evening*, was painted in 1663 for Bishop
Halmale in Antwerp. *Noon* may have been executed for the same patron. The figures were painted
by the Italian artist Philippo Lauri.
A replica commissioned by Canse (?) in 1675 is
now in the Dulwich Gallery, England. There is
a smaller copy by Ranucci now at Mans. The
Cleveland Museum of Fine Arts possesses a version
of the same landscape in which all the figures are
reproduced exactly.
The *Liber Veritatis* drawing No 154.
Preparatory drawings, which differ slightly from
the final version, are in the Albertina, Vienna, and
in the British Museum.
The *Liber Veritatis* drawing after the Hermitage
Noon is dated 1661. Because of this, Rothlisberger

suggests that the date on the Hermitage picture
should be read as 1661.

In the eighteenth century the picture was in the
gallery of the Landgrave of Hesse at Cassel. In 1806
it was taken to Paris at the order of Napoleon, and
placed in the collection of the Empress Josephine
at Malmaison, whence it came to the Hermitage
in 1815.

Literature:
Cat. 1916, No 1429; Cat. 1958, I, p. 305, No 1235;
M. Patisson, *Claude Lorrain*, Paris, 1884, pp. 220, 245;
W. Friedländer, *Claude Lorrain*, Berlin, 1926, p. 90,
96; W. Weisbach, *Die französische Malerei*, Berlin,
1932, pp. 319, 320; W. Rothlisberger, *Claude Lorrain*, 1961, p. 362.

62 LAURENT DE LA HYRE
(1606–1656)

MERCURY ENTRUSTING THE INFANT
BACCHUS TO THE NYMPHS
oil on canvas, 125 × 133 cm

Signed and dated at bottom left: *L. de la Hyre F.*
1638

Mercury, the messenger of the gods, entrusts the nymphs with the infant Bacchus, the son of Jupiter and Semele and the future god of wine and fertility, to save him from the anger of Juno, Jupiter's spouse; the nymphs are to feed the boy and watch over him. The subject is taken from Ovid's *Metamorphoses* (Book III, 314, 315).
This work is very characteristic of the style of La Hyre's easel paintings. It is executed with great superficial brilliance. The gay colours, which are bright and clear, show the influence of the Venetian school on La Hyre. But La Hyre also imitates Poussin by decorating the landscape with classical ruins. The most interesting part of the picture is the landscape background, which is one of the earliest landscapes with ruins in French art; it is bathed in a light transparent mist and anticipates the romantic landscapes of the eighteenth century.

Acquired for the Hermitage in 1772 with the Crozat Collection, Paris.

Literature:
Cat. 1903, No 1460; Cat. 1958, I, p. 291, No 1173; Réau, No 156; A. N. Benois, *Istoriya zhivopisi*, IV, Petrograd, pp. 209, 210; A. Blunt, *Art and Architecture in France 1500–1700*, London, 1953, p. 172; Ch. Sterling, *Musée de l'Ermitage. La peinture française*, Paris, 1957, p. 25.

63 SEBASTIEN BOURDON
(1616–1671)

THE DEATH OF DIDO
oil on canvas, 158 × 136.5 cm

The picture illustrates an episode from Virgil's
Aeneid (Book IV, 665–705). Dido, the Queen of Carthage, is abandoned by Aeneas, and dies on the
funeral pyre, having killed herself with a sword.
The colour scheme of the canvas, with the masterly
combination of warm golden tones with cool blue
ones and the pearly and silvery tints of the armour
on the foreground figures, shows Bourdon's interest
in the work of the Venetian school. It also suggests
that the picture should be dated to the period from
the late 1630s to the early 1640s, after the artist's
return to France from Venice, where he had stayed
for some time. The blue sea, with the receding
white sails of Aeneas's ships in the distance, is
painted with deep poetic feeling.
An engraving after the picture was made by J. R.
Michel.
An engraving from a version of this subject was
executed by Heylbrouck in 1713 when the version
was in the collection of the Duke of Devonshire.

Acquired for the Hermitage in 1772 with the Crozat
Collection, Paris.

Literature:
Cat. 1903, No 1421; Cat. 1958, I, p. 260, No 1247;
Ch. Sterling, *Musée de L'Ermitage. La peinture fran-
çaise*, Paris, 1957, p. 28.

64   PIERRE MIGNARD (?)
         (1612–1695)

PORTRAIT OF HORTENSE MANCINI
oil on canvas, 80×65 cm

The portrait was painted in the 1660s. Hortense Mancini (1640–1699) was the niece of Cardinal Mazarin and the sister of Marie Mancini, Louis XIV's famous favourite. The lady represented in this picture is close to the sitter in the portrait of Hortense Mancini painted by Peter Lely (engraved by G. Valck, 1678). The work is attributed to Mignard on stylistic grounds, for it is very characteristic of the type of formal court female portraiture practised by Mignard which was much in vogue with the public of his day. The celebrated portraitist made his models appear majestic and imposing, yet not devoid of a certain feminine charm; they are haughty and aloof as becomes ladies of high birth, but a certain languor lurks in the expression of the eyes and the mouth. Mignard is celebrated for his elaborate treatment of the details of dress and accessories, which he painted with greater freedom than he did the faces of the sitters. The embroidery in the Hermitage portrait is masterly in execution, as are the flowers which adorn the front of the model's dress, and which are worn in her hair. But if we compare the Hermitage portrait with other famous paintings by Mignard, such as the *Portrait of Marie Mancini* in Berlin and the *Portrait of the Duchesse de Lavallière* in

Marseilles, we find that the Hermitage picture lacks the virtuousity of technique, the lightness of touch and the superficial brilliance of execution which characterize the authenticated works of this great painter; it is for this reason that there are serious doubts about the attribution of this picture to Mignard. It ist most probably by Jacob Ferdinand Voet, a painter of Flemish origin who worked in Paris and in Rome, closely imitating Mignard, but whose *œuvre* is little studied (he was born in Antwerp in 1639 and was a member of the Paris Academy after 1664).

Acquired by the Hermitage in 1923 from the collection of E. P. and M. S. Olive, Petrograd.

Literature:
Cat. 1958, I, p. 310, No 743; A. Trubnikov, 'Sobraniye E. P. i M. S. Olive', *Starye Gody*, 1916 (April-June), p. 9; S. Ernst, 'Exposition de la peinture française des XVII–XVIII s. au Musée de l'Ermitage', *Gazette des Beaux-Arts*, Paris, 1928, I, p. 166; Ch. Sterling, *Musée de l'Ermitage. La peinture française*, Paris, 1957, p. 217, note 57.

65 NICOLAS DE LARGILLIÈRE
(1656–1746)

PREPARATIONS FOR THE GALA BANQUET
OF JANUARY 30th, 1687, IN THE PARIS
CITY HALL
oil on canvas, 68 × 101 cm

This work, which was painted in 1687, is a pre-paratory sketch in oils for the large canvas which Largillière executed in 1687 for one of the rooms in the Paris City Hall. The picture was destroyed between 1789 and 1794 during the Revolution. Two more sketches for the same painting are known, both smaller than the Hermitage sketch—one is in the Louvre (Cat. No 481) and the other is in the Amiens Museum.

The painting is a typical formal French portrait of the second half of the seventeenth century, a type of painting in which Largillière excelled. He pain-ted portraits of groups and individuals and in ac-cordance with the taste of the time gave his sitters an imposing and dignified air. The huge wigs form a sort of aura around their heads, the gorgeous mantles which fall from their shoulders envelop the figures and the gestures and poses are studiously majestic. The City Councillors wished to be shown discussing a plan for a banquet to be given in honour of Louis XIV, recently recovered from an illness. One of them holds a model of a monument dedicated to the monarch, the work of the sculptor Coysevox, which was soon to be installed in the Paris City Hall.

Largillière was a masterly colourist. He excelled in catching the textures of materials by his use of colour. This is shown in the treatment of the silks and velvets of the rich mantles, the locks of the fluffy wigs and the gleam of bronze in the bust.

Acquired for the Hermitage in 1772 with the Crozat Collection, Paris.

Literature:
Cat. 1903, No 1537; Cat. 1958, I, p. 297, No 1269; Pascal, *Largillière*, Paris, No 201; P. Marcel, *La peinture française au début du XVIIIᵉ siècle*, Paris, p. 212.

66 ANTOINE WATTEAU
(1684–1721)

THE SAVOYARD
oil on canvas, 40.5×32.5 cm

Watteau, who was one of the outstanding French masters of the first half of the eighteenth century, contributed a series of new themes (military scenes, scenes of daily life, *fêtes galantes*) to the art of his day, and introduced a new approach to the subject matter. All the preparatory studies for his pictures were made directly from life. He was a brilliant colourist who worked in a palette of the greatest richness and refinement.

During the period 1713–1716 Watteau produced a large group of pictures devoted to the life of the poor. Outstanding among them is this small canvas, *The Savoyard*. It is one of the best genre scenes ever painted by Watteau.

There is another version of the theme, *The Savoyard with a Saddle*, which was confused with the Hermitage picture by E. Goncourt. *The Pedlar* (private collection, Lyons), which was published by J. Mathey as the earliest variant of the subject, does not seem to be by Watteau. A drawing for *The Savoyard* by Watteau (reversed; charcoal and red chalk) is now in the Museum of the École des Beaux Arts, Paris. A landscape which is very close to the background of the *Savoyard* occurs in a drawing (red chalk and wash) in the Taylor Museum, Haarlem.

An engraving of the painting was made by B. Audran, on the same sheet as the *Woman Spinning*, the companion to *The Savoyard*, which has since been lost.

The Savoyard was for a long time thought to have been painted in 1709–1710, or at an even earlier date. H. Zimmerman and V. Josz assign it to 1707–1708. H. Adhémar suggests 1703–1708 as the period during which it may have been produced. Ch. Sterling dates the picture to 1709–1710; J. Mathey to *c.* 1713; I. Nemilova to 1716.

In the eighteenth century *The Savoyard* was in the collection of Cl. Audran. It was acquired for the Hermitage after 1774.
Exhibited at the 1937 Exhibition of Masterpieces of French Painting in Paris.

Literature:
Cat. 1903, No 1502; Cat. 1958, I, p. 266, No 1148; *Catalogue of the 1937 Exhibition*, No 226; E. de Goncourt, *Catalogue raisonné de l'œuvre peinte et gravée d'Antoine Watteau*, Paris, 1875, No 85; *Archives de l'art français*, Paris, 1888, p. 64; V. Josz, *Watteau, mœurs de XVIIIe s.*, Paris, 1903, p. 93; E. H. Zimmerman, *A. Watteau*, Stuttgart-Leipzig, 1917, p. 1; E. Dacier and A. Vuaflart, *Jean de Jullienne et les graveurs de Watteau au XVIIIe s.*, Paris, 1924, No 122; L. Réau, 'A. Watteau', *Les peintres français du XVIIIe s.* (ed. L. Dimier), I, 1928, No 164; K. T. Parker, *The Drawings of A. Watteau*, London, 1931, pl. X; V. N. Volskaya, *A. Watteau*, Moscow, 1933, p. 32; J. Brinckmann, *A. Watteau*, Vienna, 1943, p. 15; J. Mathey, 'Landscape by Watteau', *The Burlington Magazine*, 1947 (October), p. 6; H. Adhémar, *Watteau*, Paris, 1950, No 13, pp. 36, 50, 143, 144; J. Mathey and K. Parker, *Dessins de Watteau*, I, Paris, 1957, No 490, pp. 65–67, pl. XII; Ch. Sterling, *Musée de l'Ermitage. La peinture française*, Paris, 1957, p. 37; J. Mathey, *Antoine Watteau. Peintures réapparues, etc.*, Paris, 1959, pp. 24, 67, 74; E. F. Kozhina, 'Antoine Watteau. K 275-letiyu so dnya rozhdeniya', *Iskusstvo*, 1960, No 1, p. 68; I. S. Nemilova, *A. Watteau*, Moscow-Leningrad, 1961, p. 4; I. S. Nemilova, *Watteau i yego proizvedeniya v Ermitazhe*, Leningrad, 1964, pp. 100–110, Cat. No 6; I. S. Nemilova, 'Kartina Watteau "Savoyard" i problema periodizatsii tvorchestva khudozhnika', *Trudy Gosudarstvennogo Ermitazha*, VIII, 1965, pp. 182–184.

67 ANTOINE WATTEAU
(1684–1721)

THE EMBARRASSING PROPOSAL
oil on canvas, 65 × 84.5 cm

Antoine Watteau created a new genre, the *fêtes galantes*. These are scenes of entertainment in the open air, concerts on the edge of mysteriously dense parkland, dances in glades of wild flowers, or elegant ladies and gentlemen conversing under old trees in quiet walks.

The Embarrassing Proposal is a *fête galante*. It shows a party resting in the shadow of some trees in a valley which is filled with light and air. The main characters, the young beau and his lady, stand somewhat apart from the rest of the party. The young man is arguing with his companion and pressing his point heatedly and impetuously; she is obviously offended by his proposal, for her small head is tossed back haughtily and she has picked up her skirt and is about to retire in anger. The two young women sitting on the grass are deeply absorbed in their conversation and quite unconscious of what is going on. But the young man lolling on the ground near them watches the ripening quarrel with close and ironic attention and seems to find it all most amusing. All the nuances of these feelings, which are almost imperceptible but infinitely varied, were first painted by Watteau.

The Embarrassing Proposal is a rare example of a painting by Watteau in a beautiful state of preservation. Because of the master's constant experiments with pigments, many of his pictures have shrunk and darkened. *The Embarrassing Proposal* retains all its original freshness and brightness of colour.

The surface of the canvas shows differences in the thickness of the paint which are due to the changes which Watteau made as he worked. The lower paint layers show through the overpainting in places. X-rays confirm the results of visual observation and show that in the right foreground there was originally a clump of trees and some shrubs, to balance those on the left of the picture. They were overpainted, to achieve a greater effect of depth and space. The arrangement of the figures in the group on the left has been completely changed. The girl playing a guitar had originally been painted almost full face, after the drawing No 57 in the catalogue of K. T. Parker and J. Mathey.

The related picture is *Le Plaisir Pastoral* in the Condé Museum, Chantilly.

Drawings for *The Embarrassing Proposal* have survived. One, for the figure of the girl musician, shows her in three different attitudes (charcoal, red chalk, lead pencil; Paris, Louvre); it was used in *The Pleasures of Life* (Wallace Collection, London). Another drawing, for the lady seated with her back to the viewer (reversed; red chalk), is in Amsterdam. The figure in the picture seems to be done after the contre-épreuve in the Baron de Shwiter Collection, sold in 1863 (Lot 179). There is a drawing for the young man standing to the right (red chalk) in the Lyon Collection, London. An engraving of the picture was made by N. Tardieu for the *Récueil* of Jullienne, with the inscription: *La proposition embarassante*. Another was made

68 ANTOINE WATTEAU
(1684–1721)

THE EMBARRASSING PROPOSAL
(Detail)

by M. Keyl for the volume of engravings from pictures in the Brühl Collection.
The work was painted about 1716 (H. Adhémar gives the same date; J. Mathey gives 1715).

Acquired for the Hermitage in 1769 with the Brühl Collection.

Literature:
Cat. 1903; No 1501; Cat. 1958, I, p. 266, No 1150; *Récueil d'Estampes gravées d'après les tableaux de la Galerie et du Cabinet de S. E. M. le Comte de Brühl, à Dresde*, 1754; E. Goncourt, *Catalogue raisonné de l'œuvre peinte et gravée d'A. Watteau*, Paris, 1875, No 152; E. H. Zimmermann, *A. Watteau*, Stuttgart-Leipzig, 1917, p. XX; E. Dacier and A. Vuaflart, *Jean de Jullienne et les graveurs de Watteau au XVIIIe siècle*, Paris, 1924, No 244; L. Réau, 'A. Watteau', *Les peintres français du XVIIIe s.* (ed. L. Dimier), I, 1928, No 129; V. N. Volskaya, *Watteau*, Moscow, 1933, p. 32; H. Adhémar, *Watteau*, Paris, 1930, No 142, p. 144; K. T. Parker and J. Mathey, *Antoine Watteau, Catalogue complet de son œuvre dessinée*, II, Paris, 1957, Nos 636, 643, 825; Ch. Sterling, *Le Musée de l'Ermitage. La peinture française*, Paris, 1957, p. 40; J. Mathey, *A. Watteau. Peintures réapparues etc.*, Paris, 1959, p. 68; I. S. Nemilova, *A. Watteau*, Moscow-Leningrad, 1961, pl. 17; I. S. Nemilova, *Watteau i yego proizvedeniya v Ermitazhe*, Leningrad, 1964, pp. 130–138, Cat. No 5.

69 ANTOINE WATTEAU
(1684–1721)

THE CAPRICIOUS GIRL (LA BOUDEUSE)
oil on canvas, 42×34 cm

Like *The Embarrassing Proposal, The Capricious Girl* is a *fête galante*. Its simple story is like that of *The Embarrassing Proposal*. During a walk in the park, a young couple in search of solitude has broken away from the rest of the party. The young beau is lounging freely and unceremoniously behind the girl on the stone bench on which she is sitting and is evidently annoying her by talking malicious nonsense. The characters are freshly and subtly observed. The master has caught beautifully the self-confidence of the conceited young rake, and the entire range of complicated emotions which are agitating the lady. She is provoked almost beyond endurance by the ironic remarks of her companion, whom she cannot check; and she seems unable even to decide whether she ought to treat his remarks as a joke and laugh with him or to take offence and retire. Her silly little face reflects all the strain which the unaccustomed situation, too complex for her to cope with, has put upon her. There is a similar situation in *The Embarrassing Proposal*, but there the emotional atmosphere is quite different. This difference is characteristic of Watteau, who could endlessly vary a given theme and invest it each time with a different gamut of subtle emotions.

The Capricious Girl is one of the pictures from Watteau's last period in the Hermitage collection. On stylistic grounds it may be dated *c.* 1718.

There is an engraving of the picture made by P. Mercier for Jullienne's volume of engravings; it is entitled *La Boudeuse*.

In the eighteenth century and the first half of the nineteenth century the canvas was in the collection of Horace Walpole at Strawberry Hill, Twickenham, England. It was acquired by P. C. Stroganov in the mid-nineteenth century, and came to the Hermitage in 1923.

Literature:
Cat. 1958, I, p. 270. J. P. Mariette, *Le manuscrit du Cabinet d'Estampes de la Bibliothèque Nationale*, IX, 1921; E. Goncourt, *Catalogue raisonné de l'œuvre peinte, dessinée et gravée d'Antoine Watteau*, Paris, 1875; L. de Fourcaud, 'A. Watteau', *Revue de l'Art ancien et moderne*, 1904, XVI (July-September), p. 356; E. H. Zimmermann, *A. Watteau*, Stuttgart-Leipzig, 1917, No 84; V. F. Miller, 'Frantsuzskaya zhivopis XVII–XVIII vv. v novykh zalakh Ermitazha', *Gorod*, 1923, No 1, p. 59; E. Dacier and A. Vuaflart, *Jean de Jullienne et les graveurs de Watteau au XVIIIe s.*, Paris, 1924, No 303; L. Réau 'A. Watteau', *Les peintres du XVIIIe s.* (ed. L. Dimier), I, 1928, No 101; S. Ernst, 'L'exposition de peinture française des XVII–XVIII s. au Musée de l'Ermitage', *Gazette des Beaux-Arts*, 1928, I, p. 171; V. N. Volskaya, *A. Watteau*, Moscow, 1933, p. 27; H. Adhémar, *Watteau*, Paris, 1950, No 220; K. T. Parker and J. Mathey, *Antoine Watteau. Catalogue complet de son œuvre dessinée*, II, Paris, 1957, No 749; I. S. Nemilova, *A. Watteau*, Moscow-Leningrad, 1961, p. 9; I. S. Nemilova, *Watteau i yego proizvedeniya v Ermitazhe*, Leningrad, 1964, pp. 146–151, Cat. No 7.

70 NICOLAS LANCRET
(1690–1743)

PORTRAIT OF THE DANCER CAMARGO
oil on canvas, 45×55 cm

Nicolas Lancret was one of the best-known and most successful followers of Watteau. Like Watteau, Lancret painted *galante* and theatrical scenes, and small pictures with scenes of everyday life. Most of these works were unimaginative imitations; and it is not through them that Lancret won recognition as a painter. His reputation rests upon his portraits of people from the world of the theatre. In contrast with Watteau, who when he painted the actors of his acquaintance carefully isolated them from the atmosphere of the play and set the figures against an imaginative background, Lancret painted actors standing on the stage, surrounded by the scenery and the costumes connected with their performance.

His portraits of the two most brilliant dancers of his day, Mlle Camargo and Mlle Sallé, contributed greatly to Lancret's fame. The Hermitage canvas represents Mlle Marie-Anne Cuppi de Camargo (1710–1770), the celebrated ballerina and one of the cleverest, most gifted and best-informed women of the time. She was much admired by ballet-lovers in fashionable society, and she was also on friendly terms with Grimm and Helvetius, philosophers of the Enlightenment, and Voltaire dedicated poems to her. Mlle Camargo made a number of innovations in the art of ballet, making certain changes in the costume and shortening the skirt. This was to prove an important advance in the development of the art.

There are four versions of the portrait of Mlle Camargo by Lancret. Beside the one in the Hermitage there are three others, one in the Museum of Nantes (No 127), another in the Wallace Collection (No 393) and the third in the New Palace at Potsdam (No 65). The first three versions are almost identical and differ only in the colour of the dress, which is golden in the Hermitage painting and light blue in the other two. The Potsdam version shows Mlle Camargo with a partner.

A drawing of Mlle Camargo which differs from each of the four versions is in the Louvre (No 5622). More than fifteen replicas and copies of this composition were recorded in the various sales held in the course of the nineteenth century.

Acquired for the Hermitage between 1763 and 1774.

Literature:
Cat. 1903, No 1883; Cat. 1958, I, p. 296, No 1145; Clement de Ris, 'Les Musées du Nord. Le Musée impérial de l'Ermitage à S. Petersbourg', *Gazette des Beaux-Arts*, 1880, XXI, p. 269; J. J. Guiffrey (Publisher), Ballot de Sovot, *Eloge de Lancret, peintre du roi*, Paris, pp. 67–69, 71–74; E. Dacier, 'A propos du portrait de la Camargo par Lancret', *Musées de France*, 1911, No 3, p. 42; E. Dacier, 'Les portraits gravés de la Camargo', *Revue de l'art ancien et moderne*, 1911, VII, p. 143; E. Davier, *Une danseuse de l'Opéra sous Louis XV. Mlle Sallé, etc.*, Paris, 1909, pp. 83–87, 104, 105, 118; G. Wildenstein, *Lancret*, Paris, No 584, pp. 109, 110; F. I. Blinov, *Tantsovshchitsa Camargo*, Leningrad, 1948.

71

FRANÇOIS BOUCHER
(1703–1770)

LANDSCAPE NEAR BEAUVAIS
oil on canvas, 49×58 cm

The versatile genius of François Boucher, the celebrated French master, found expression in many types of painting, but in none more fully or extensively than in decorative paintings. He painted ceilings and medallions for the interiors of elegant houses, designed interior decorations, worked as book illustrator, made cartoons for tapestries and painted fans. Some of the models for porcelain figurines produced at the famous Sèvres factory were made after his drawings. Boucher's pictures cover a wide range and include portraits, mythological scenes, compositions illustrating different episodes of Greek and Roman history, religious subjects, pastorals of studied naivety and landscapes of amazing elegance. Common to all, however, is Boucher's love of decoration.

The *Landscape near Beauvais* is one of the most notable Bouchers in the Hermitage. The landscape, as may be guessed from its title, is supposed to be realistic, but it is obvious that nature has here undergone a considerable transformation, for the composition is like a décor for a ballet set in fairyland, or for a pastoral opera. The foreground, with the pond, the boat moored at the bank and the heavy stone slabs, seems to be designed for the theatre. The bridge, the steps and the balcony in the background might have been placed there to give room for the actors. The soft shimmering light, the transparent blue mist enveloping the distance and the graceful shapes of the slender trees with the tops soaring upwards seem to have been conceived by the poetic imagination of the author rather than observed from nature. The landscape is enlivened by several small figures painted in a very lively, though somewhat mannered style; there is a girl on the balcony of the pigeon-house, another girl in a boat, rinsing clothes in the pond, and a young boy stands by her side. His red clothes provide a bright spot in the otherwise greenish tonality of the painting; there is a more subdued tone in the dress of the young laundress, and the touches of pink in the pale-blue sky strike a note of gaiety which further enhances the delicacy and refinement of the colour scheme.

Nevertheless, this imaginative landscape records some of the artist's impressions of Beauvais. Boucher used to visit the town and its neighbourhood between 1734 and 1755 when he was connected with the local tapestry factory, for which he executed cartoons and drawings. There are some sketches of a place which looks somewhat like the Hermitage landscape in the Rijksmuseum, Amsterdam, and the Munich Pinakothek. Van Regteren Altena considers the Munich study to be the most accurate topographically, while in the others nature seems to have been idealized.

This painting was exhibited in the Salon of 1742 with the title *Une vue des environs de Beauvais*. The *œuvre* of Boucher includes several landscape paintings in the same vein, which incorporate the same

72

FRANÇOIS BOUCHER
(1703–1770)

LANDSCAPE NEAR BEAUVAIS
(Detail)

buildings, including the *Landscape with a Water Mill* (the Salon, 1740), the *Landscape with a Water Mill and a Woman feeding Poultry in the Foreground* (the Salon, 1743), and some others.

An engraving of the picture was made by N. F. Le Bas in 1744; it is reversed, and has the same title as in the Salon. There is also a companion picture of the same view, the *Deuxième vue des environs de Beauvais*.

In the mid-nineteenth century the picture was in the Lenoir Collection; in the early twentieth century it had passed to the Olive Collection. It was acquired by the Hermitage in 1923, was transferred to the State Pushkin Museum of Fine Arts, Moscow, in 1925, and was returned to the Hermitage in 1930.

Literature:
Cat. 1958, I, p. 261, No 5743; L. Auvray, *Dictionnaire général des Artistes de l'école française*, I, Paris, 1882, p. 129; A. Michel, *F. Boucher*, Paris, p. 54; A. N. Benois, *Istoriya zhivopisi*, IV, Petrograd, p. 332, note 217; A. Trubnikov and S. Ernst, 'Sobraniye E. P. i M. S. Olive', *Starye Gody*, 1916 (April-June), pp. 6–8; J. O. van Regteren Altena, 'Het landscap bij Beauvais van F. Boucher', *Bulletin van het Rijksmuseum*, 1959, No 2, pp. 27–31; *Le dessin français dans les collections hollandaises*, Paris-Amsterdam, 1964, p. 68, pl. 82, No 66.

73 FRANÇOIS BOUCHER
(1703–1770)

LANDSCAPE WITH A POND
oil on canvas, 51 × 65 cm

Signed and dated at bottom right: *F. Boucher 1746*

This splendidly executed picture shows Boucher's landscape painting at its best. Like most other pictures from this period of the master's career, it is based on studies from nature which have been transformed, in the process of artistic re-creation, into an imaginative landscape. Not only the shapes and character of all the objects, but their very colours have been transformed. The prevailing tonality in this picture is greenish blue, and the view has the refined quality of theatrical scenery. The cool silvery background tone is relieved by the bright red in the dress of the young boy; Boucher repeated this effect in a number of his later pictures. The statue on the left of the composition was often painted by the master and can be seen in *The Tame Sparrow* and in the Hermitage *Fording the River*.

Acquired between 1763 and 1774. Transferred to the Hermitage from the Gatchina Castle in 1882.

Literature:
Cat. 1916, No 1797; Cat. 1958, I, p. 261, No 1137; Ch. Sterling, *Musée de l'Ermitage. La peinture française*, Paris, 1957, p. 46.

74   FRANÇOIS BOUCHER
(1703–1770)

LANDSCAPE WITH A POND
(Detail)

75 JEAN-BAPTISTE PERRONNEAU
(1715–1783)

PORTRAIT OF A BOY WITH A BOOK
oil on canvas, 63×52 cm

Art-historians who study French eighteenth-century art are particularly interested in the portraiture of the period. Two schools of portrait painting can be distinguished: the old realistic tradition, which is represented by such masters as M. de La Tour, J.-B. Perronneau, B. Lépicié and S. Chardin; and the tradition of official court portraits which was elaborated by J. M. Nattier, F. Boucher and E. Vigée-Lebrun. Each of these schools developed independently until the French Revolution, and each in turn gained ascendance. Perronneau was one of the leading artists of the realistic school. The Hermitage *Boy with a Book* is one of his masterpieces. The fragile child with a thin transparent face and large questioning eyes is painted with extraordinary vividness. Even in the childish face of his young sitter Perronneau saw much that deserved to be taken seriously, and painted these features in his portrait. If we recall the plump, round-cheeked, pink amoretti which did duty for children in the paintings of Perronneau's contemporaries, his approach to the subject will seem particularly striking, as it must have done to the viewer of his day. The identity of the sitter is still uncertain. In the list of Perronneau's canvases exhibited in the Salon of 1746, 'a portrait in oils representing a schoolboy with a book, a brother of the artist' (No 150) is mentioned. This is probably identified with the Hermitage picture. Perronneau's *œuvre* includes one more picture of a boy with a book; it is a pastel which was owned at the end of the nineteenth century by Jacques Doucet. We do not know how close the Hermitage painting is to the pastel. The dating of the Hermitage canvas to 1745–1746 is supported by a comparison of this work with the portrait of Jean-Baptiste-Antoine Lemoine as a child, which is securely dated to 1747 (now in a private collection).

The attribution of the portrait has a long and complicated history. It was originally attributed to J. B. Greuze (see Neustroyev, 1898, and Cat. 1900). Wrangel published it as a work by J. B. Lépicié, giving no proofs to support his attribution. His view was accepted by F. Ingersoll-Smouse and later by G. Wildenstein; Weiner was the first to publish the portrait as the work of J.-B. Perronneau. L. Vaillat, in a revised edition of his book, accepted his opinion; so did Ratouis de Limay.

The replica in the Hulot Collection, Paris, is regarded by Wildenstein as a copy made by Chardin.

Acquired for the Hermitage at the end of the eighteenth century from the collection of G. N. Teplov.

Literature:
Cat. 1900, No 1519 (Greuze); Cat. 1916, No 1519 (Perronneau); Cat. 1958, I, p. 324, No 1270; A. A. Neustroyev, *Imperatorskaya kartinnaya galereya Ermitazha*, Saint Petersburg, 1898, p. 344, No 1519; G. K. Nagler, *Neues Allgemeines Künstler-Lexicon*, II, Munich, 1841, p. 116; N. Wrangel, *Les chefs-d'œuvre de la Galerie de tableaux de l'Ermitage Impérial à St Pétersbourg*, London-Munich-New York, pp. XXIII, XXVII; P. Weiner, *Chefs-d'œuvre de la Galerie des tableaux de l'Ermitage*, Munich, 1923, p. 30; L. Vaillat, *J.-B. Perronneau, sa vie et son œuvre*, Paris, pp. 3–5, 9; G. Wildenstein, *Chardin*, Paris, 1921, No 629, pl. 206, p. 202.

76

JEAN-BAPTISTE-SIMÉON CHARDIN
(1699–1779)

THE WASHERWOMAN
oil on canvas, 37.5×42.7 cm

Chardin is one of the outstanding masters of the realistic school in French eighteenth-century painting, but he did not exert a revolutionary influence upon the art of his day. His work does not seem to undermine the foundations of tradition. He paints merely what he sees, and what he knows intimately. His ideal of human existence is the way of life of the French petty bourgeois and many of his works show us women at home, enjoying the daily tasks of caring for the house and the family. This was the ideal which he set up in opposition to the empty, thoughtless personages of contemporary aristocratic art. And this is the spirit in which the master treats his favourite theme in *The Washerwoman*, painted *c.* 1737. The scene is set in an almost dark room. A young woman is washing clothes and bends over a large wooden tub which is full of soap-suds. A rosy-cheeked child sits on a low chair near her; he is blowing bubbles with a straw. There are only a few simple objects in the room: the tub, a wooden chair, a ladder propped against the wall in the corner and the thick pottery bowl on the floor. The young washerwoman wears a cap with long side pieces, a loose striped blouse and a white apron—the normal dress of a city woman of modest means. The boy's clothes, which are much too big for him, probably belonged to an elder brother who has outgrown them. The composition of the scene is very simple. The group of the mother and the boy is placed in the centre but they have been moved slightly to the left in order to make room for the girl who is seen through the open door in the background. Her figure and the lighted space in which she stands are used to counterbalance the figure of the washerwoman. The contents of the room are arranged almost symmetrically. The colour and lighting is carefully arranged in a pattern in which the brightest colour and the strongest light are concentrated on the figure of the boy, and the two women on either side of him are placed in a light of almost equal intensity; behind them the background is darkened so that the neutral colours stand out against it. The composition and the distribution of light are clear and logical, and harmonize with the subject of the painting. The perfect rhythm and balance of the arrangement of the individual components of the scene create a mood of tranquillity, and even suggest the silence in the room. The attention of the viewer does not wander aimlessly over the picture, but passes logically from object to object. This is not the only way, however, in which the painter achieved the desired effect. The merry, healthy child absorbed in his play, the large spotted tom-cat which is purring almost audibly and the kind, pretty face of the woman add to the mood of domestic peace and comfort.

The Washerwoman is the replica of a picture exhibited in the Salon of 1737, which was engraved in 1739 by C. N. Cochin. A picture of the same theme, shown at the Salon in 1739 together with its companion, was in the La Roque sale of 1745. A third version is now in Stockholm, it is signed *Chardin* on the left, and has the monogram *S. C.*

77

JEAN-BAPTISTE-SIMÉON CHARDIN
(1699–1779)

THE WASHERWOMAN
(Detail)

in the corner of the washerwoman's apron (an engraving was made from this picture by Gusman,
after a drawing by Bocourt); in the literature on
Chardin, this version is frequently said to have
belonged to La Roque. Wildenstein regards the
Hermitage painting as a replica of the Stockholm
picture, because the signature on the apron is
found in both. However, there is no monogram in
the Hermitage canvas. It differs from the other
versions in that there is no straw on the floor at the
right. The replica owned by Sir Herbert Cook, of
Richmond, seems to have been copied from the
Hermitage painting. E. de Rothschild also possesses
a picture of the same subject. The canvas listed in
the inventory of the artist's property made after
his death, was last recorded in the Lefèvre sale of
1897 (Lot 236). Over fifteen pictures of this subject
appeared in different sales in the course of the nineteenth century; it is not clear which of these were
autograph replicas and which merely copies.

Acquired for the Hermitage with the Crozat Collection (Cat. 1755, p. 55; where the size of the
canvas is given incorrectly as: 0.37×0.24).

Literature:
Cat. 1903, No 1514; Cat. 1958, I, p. 335, No 1185;
G. Wildenstein, *Chardin*, Paris, 1933, No 5; V. Lasareff, *Chardin*, Moscow, 1947, pp. 30, 31; I. S. Nemilova, *Siméon Chardin i yego kartiny v Gosudarstvennom Ermitazhe*, Leningrad, 1961, pp. 5–7.

78 JEAN-BAPTISTE-SIMÉON CHARDIN
(1699–1779)

GRACE BEFORE A MEAL (LE BÉNÉDICITÉ)
oil on canvas, 49.5×38.4 cm

Signed and dated in the background at the left: *Chardin 1744;* fake signature at bottom left: *Chardin*

In Chardin's attitude towards the characters in his paintings there was no room for indifference. He was not content with mere photographic representation of scenes from family life, but showed great warmth and affection, and even a certain pride, in his treatment of his characters. *Le Bénédicité* shows this side of the master. His sympathy for the three characters in the picture is obvious.

The composition is carefully planned to enhance the expressive quality of the painting. The figures are arranged around the table in the centre of the canvas where the light is strongest, and all the action is confined to this space. The composition, which has been carefully worked out in all its details, reflects the author's conception of the family as a closely knit group, and reveals the ties which link its members. *Grace before a Meal* is one of Chardin's favourite subjects. He exhibited works of this theme three times, in the Salons of 1740 (No 61), of 1746 (No 71) and of 1761 (No 42). The 1740 version is now in the Louvre. There are several engravings, which were probably made from this first version. As the Hermitage painting is the only version to be signed and dated, even if it is not the first to have been executed, it was evidently recognized by the author as the best or the most important version. It differs from the other versions in having a pan

with some eggs in it in the foreground, and a plain instead of a checkered floor.

Several versions of *Le Bénédicité* are known: a canvas in the Louvre (probably identical with the picture listed in the inventory of the artist's property made after his death), a panel in the collection of Lord Wemyss, Scotland, an interesting variant with an oblong format in the Abdy Collection (with a larger interior and the figure of a boy servant carrying a dish, there is a drawing after this version by St Oben), and a painting in the Veil-Picard Collection, Paris (which also includes a number of important changes). The Stockholm version has an inscription on the back, which says that the picture is a copy finished by Chardin.

Some more versions were recorded in various sales in the eighteenth and nineteenth centuries.

Acquired for the Hermitage between 1763 and 1774.

Literature:
Cat. 1903, No 1513; Cat. 1958, I, p. 355, No 1193; G. Wildenstein, *Chardin*, Paris, 1933, Cat. No 78; V. Lasareff, *Chardin*, Moscow, 1947, p. 4; Ch. Sterling, *Musée de l'Ermitage. La peinture française*, Paris, 1957, pp. 43, 217; I. S. Nemilova, *Siméon Chardin i yego kartiny v Gosudarstvennom Ermitazhe*, Leningrad, 1961, pp. 8, 9.

JEAN-BAPTISTE-SIMÉON CHARDIN
(1699–1779)

STILL-LIFE WITH THE ATTRIBUTES
OF THE ARTS
oil on canvas, 112×140.5 cm

Signed and dated at bottom left, on the edge of the table: *Chardin 1766*

Chardin was in many respects an innovator in still-life painting. He had a new conception of this genre, which was influenced by the philosophy of the Enlightenment, and in his treatment of the subject expressed the new outlook of the period which immediately preceded the French Revolution.

Chardin's still-lives suggest the personality of the owner, which is felt in each individual object. Man is the owner, the creator and the user of things. An idea of his tastes and aspirations can be gained through looking at his belongings.

The still-life in question, which was originally called *Les Attributs des arts et leur récompense*, shows an artist's table on which are arranged in a seemingly haphazard fashion various objects directly or indirectly connected with painting, sculpture and architecture. In the centre of the composition is *Mercury*, a plaster statuette by Pigalle, which, together with the vessel decorated with a chased ornament to the right, represents sculpture. The art of painting is symbolized by a palette and a paint-box; architecture by rolls of draughts and a case of drawing instruments. The cross of the Order of St Michael, on a sash with a bow, and a few medals gained at exhibitions show us the rewards of the painter. Even when Chardin painted an allegorical composition, he painted every object directly from life, making

skilful use of colour and light to render its texture. The grey tone broken by the occasional spot of light or by a reflection from one of the surrounding objects shows the dirty plaster of the statuette, while the short strokes of light paint render the metallic glint of the medals in the foreground. The generally subdued colouring fits the simple and modest character of the objects represented perfectly.

The picture was executed at the order of the Empress Catherine II for the St Petersburg Academy of Arts.

Closely related to the Hermitage picture is the still-life in the Louvre, the *Still-life with the Attributes of the Arts* (No 1133). It is earlier than the Hermitage canvas, as it was produced in 1765 for the Marquis de Marigny for the Choisy Castle, and is the first version of the composition. The Louvre picture shows the same objects as ours and the composition is also similar, although it is looser. The catalogue of the Salon of 1769 mentions a still-life which is a replica of the one in the Hermitage (it is now in the Museum of Minneapolis).

On its arrival in Russia, the picture was not sent to the Academy of Arts but remained in the Hermitage. In 1854 it was auctioned in the sale organized at the order of Nicholas I. In 1926 the canvas was returned to the Hermitage (Wildenstein is wrong when he asserts that it was in one of the imperial palaces all the time).

Literature:
Cat. 1958, I, p. 355, No 5627; N. Wrangel, 'Iskusstvo i gosudar Nikolay I', *Starye Gody*, 1913 (July-September), pp. 89, 90; L. Réau, *Catalogue de l'Art français dans les musées russes*, Paris, 1929, p. 20; G. Wildenstein, *Chardin*, Paris, 1921, No 1134; E. Nothaft, 'Attributy iskusstva i problema allegoricheskogo natyurmorta u Chardina', *Ezhegodnik Gosudarstvennogo Ermitazha*, vol. I, part 2, Leningrad, 1937, pp. 1–4; Ch. Sterling, *Musée de l'Ermitage. La peinture française*, Paris, 1957, pp. 43, 217; I. S. Nemilova, *Siméon Chardin i yego kartiny v Gosudarstvennom Ermitazhe*, Leningrad, 1961, pp. 13, 14.

80 JEAN-BAPTISTE GREUZE
(1725–1805)

HEAD OF A GIRL
oil on canvas, 41 × 33 cm

The *Head of a Girl*, painted between 1760 and 1765, illustrates perfectly Greuze's realism. It is probably a direct study from life. The slight turn of the girl's head, her childlike face and her smile have been caught on canvas most faithfully, so that the picture is extraordinarily lifelike. In this picture Greuze did not try to achieve the effect of mere outward prettiness that is so often found in his other famous 'heads'. The sincerity of Greuze's approach adds much to the human appeal of the picture.
A drawing of the same head, in a slightly different pose, is in the Albertina, Vienna.

Acquired for the Hermitage in 1768 with the Cobentzl Collection, Brussels.

Literature:
Cat. 1903, No 1517; Cat. 1958, I, p. 281, No 1254; Catalogue de Martin et Masson, *Greuze*, Paris, No 64; Ch. Sterling, *Musée de l'Ermitage. La peinture française*, Paris, 1957, p. 61.

81

HONORÉ FRAGONARD
(1732–1806)

THE SNATCHED KISS
oil on canvas, 47×60 cm

The Snatched Kiss (or, as it is called in other versions, *The Forfeit Lost*) is a very characteristic Fragonard. It is only a very free and lively sketch for a picture. The vivacity of the movement, the spontaneity of the presentation of the characters and the spirit of infectious merriment in the picture create an unforgettable impression. The excitement of the young people over the game of cards, their noisy behaviour and a certain coarseness in their manners are rendered admirably. Fragonard does not idealize the scene but paints what he saw in real life. Like Chardin, Fragonard often records the direct results of his observation of life and manners. But Chardin carefully selects from a vast mass of material the features which, in his opinion, illustrate the ideals of a sedate middle-class existence; Fragonard, on the other hand, is not interested in this type of life. He chooses the things which he finds amusing, jolly, and probably even slightly frivolous. A comparison of the work of the two painters gives us an insight into the differences of character and outlook of two social groups in pre-revolutionary France. Fragonard does not delve deep under the surface of things, and he does not analyse or digest his emotional reactions; the viewer gets his reactions, so to speak, 'piping hot'. This is the strength and the charm of Fragonard's art which is felt and appreciated even by the sophisticated modern viewer who is so hard to please.

Several pictures of the same story are known. Firstly, the Hermitage painting; secondly, the canvas which in the early twentieth century was in the Sedelmayer Collection, later in the Veil Collection, Paris, and is now in the Hetward Collection; thirdly, an identical composition in the collection of Goldschmidt-Rothschild; fourthly, the painting now in the Metropolitan Museum of Art, New York. G. Wildenstein regards the fourth version, also known as *Making up a Quarrel*, *Interior of a Room* and *The Lost Forfeit*, as the main version. It was probably painted during Fragonard's stay in Italy, for the Bailli de Breteuil. An engraving of it was made by Robert Brichet. E. and J. Goncourt suggest that the picture reveals Fragonard's interest in Murillo, but we are not prepared to accept this view.

The Hermitage picture is painted in a broad manner; there are certain differences in the figures, namely the poses of the youth and the girl, and also in the interior. The Hermitage picture is apparently a sketch for the composition of the other versions. It is a companion to the *Preparations for a Meal* or *A Poor Family*, a sketch in the State Pushkin Museum of Fine Arts in Moscow.

The picture, together with its companion, was in the Le Clerc sale of December 17th, 1764 (Lot 298); afterwards it was in the Yusupov Collection. It was acquired by the Hermitage in 1925.

Literature:
Cat. of the Yusupov Gallery, 1920, No 65; Cat. 1958, I, p. 346, No 5646; *Sokrovishcha Rossii*, 1906, IV, pp. 201, 202; *Mir iskusstv*, 1900, II, p. 150; *Der Cicerone*, 1925, part II; L. Réau, *Fragonard, sa vie et son œuvre*, Paris, 1956, p. 157; V. Zolotov, *Fragonard*, Moscow, 1959, p. 13; G. Wildenstein, *Fragonard*, Paris, 1960, p. 224, Cat. No 118.

82

HONORÉ FRAGONARD
(1732–1806)

THE STOLEN KISS
oil on canvas, 45×55 cm

The small canvas *The Stolen Kiss*, painted in the 1780s, is full of exquisite charm. The simple story is told in a happy, light-hearted manner; the youthful grace of the boy and girl who meet by accident behind the drawing-room door, the masterly execution of the picture and the sincerity of the approach at once engage the sympathies of the viewer. Fragonard worked mainly for aristocratic patrons. His *œuvre* comprises many allegorical compositions and mythological pictures, as well as love-scenes, which are sometimes very frivolous. But because he was born into the period immediately preceding the French Revolution, he felt the influence of the new ideas which were emerging with the formation of a new approach to man and his environment. This new attitude is reflected in a series of works which should properly be called genre scenes, and which are perfectly realistic in their treatment of the artist's society. *The Stolen Kiss* is one of these pictures. In this, as well as in the other paintings in the series, Fragonard followed the tradition of the Dutch school. The heroine of the painting, a slim French girl, wears a dress which might have been painted by Terborch. We can easily find prototypes in Dutch art for the softness of the woollen carpet, the broken folds of the satin and the transparency of the diaphanous shawl. The lightness and softness of the colour scheme is somewhat reminiscent of Chardin. Fragonard's treatment of details in this picture is unusually minute as he tries to achieve the greatest possible accuracy in his rendering of the textures. His usual broad, easy and full strokes are here replaced by sharp touches with a full brush which make the surface of the picture look almost like enamel.

The Hermitage painting is close to *The Contract* or *The Promise of Marriage* (whose present whereabouts are unknown) in its general character, format and treatment.

There is an engraving of the Hermitage picture by N. F. Regnault, who regarded the work as a companion to *The Bolt*, although the two pictures are not related. The impressions of the engraving have either been printed in black-and-white or in colour, or coloured with a brush.

83 HONORÉ FRAGONARD
    (1732–1806)

    THE STOLEN KISS
    (Detail)

Acquired for the Hermitage in 1895 from the Lazienky Palace, Warsaw (the collection of Stanislas August Poniatowsky).

Literature:
Ancien inventaire du Palace Lazienky, No 77; Cat. 1903, No 1845; *Cat. de l'exposition des Chefs-d'œuvre de l'art français du XVIIIᵉ siècle*, Paris, 1937, No 165; Cat. 1958, I, p. 346, No 1300; A. Laudon, 'Salon 1808', *Annales du Musée*, 1808, p. 9; Ch. Blanc, *Histoire des peintres de l'école française*, II, p. 10; E. and J. de Goncourt, 'Fragonard', *Gazette des Beaux-Arts*, 1865, I, p. 140; L. Dussieux, *Les artistes français à l'étranger*, Paris-Lyon, 1876, p. 533; R. Nevill, 'J. H. Fragonard', *The Burlington Magazine*, 1903, III, p. 290; L. de Fourcaud, 'J. H. Fragonard', *Revue d'Art*, XXI, 1907, p. 300; A. Dayot, *La peinture française au XVIIIᵉ siècle*, pp. 216–218; L. Réau, *Histoire de la peinture française au XVIIIᵉ siècle*, II, Paris, 1926, p. 28; L. Réau, *Catalogue de l'Art français dans les musées russes*, Paris, 1929, No 102; G. Grappe, *La vie et l'œuvre de J. H. Fragonard*, II, Paris, 1923, pp. 28, 86; L. Réau, *Fragonard, sa vie et son œuvre*, Paris, 1956, p. 157; A. N. Benois, *Istoriya zhivopisi*, IV, Petrograd, p. 358; Y. Zolotov, *Fragonard*, Moscow, 1959, p. 17; G. Wildenstein, *Paintings of Fragonard*, London, 1960, p. 320, No 823, pl. 124.

84 HUBERT ROBERT
(1733–1808)

THE FLIGHT
oil on canvas, 50×42 cm

Signed at bottom right: *H. Robert*

The art of Hubert Robert, who was one of the leading masters of decorative painting in the second half of the eighteenth century, reflected the growth of interest in antiquity which had been aroused by the excavations conducted in Italy. He generally painted the ruins of ancient Roman buildings with fragments of statues and remains of large architectural complexes, or the ruins of magnificent Renaissance palaces, or the parks of Marly and Versailles, which were famous for their poetic charm. The two small pictures in the Hermitage collection, *The Flight* and *The Nest Destroyers*, are very different from the master's usual type of painting. *The Flight*, which is a particularly remarkable artistic achievement, shows a young man chasing a young girl. He runs down the steps of a broken bridge, but the girl, who is running in front of him, so fast that her dress flows out behind her, is already almost hidden by the bank on which the thick silvery willows grow. The elements of the scenery of the old overgrown park, with its shady trees, the brook which rushes from under the semicircular arch of the small stone bridge over its stony bed, the bluish foliage of the willows and the light figure of the girl flitting among them like some charming vision, are all delightful to look at. The painting is filled with a mood of poetic joy. This is also true of the companion picture, *The Nest Destroyers*. The red chalk drawing now in the Valence Museum, which has the same title as the Hermitage picture, is undoubtedly a preparatory sketch for it and helps us to understand the subject of *The Flight*. There is a Latin inscription on the stone in the foreground which reads: *Et fugit ad salices et se cupit ante videri* ('She escapes to the willows, but takes care that I see her going').

This is a line from Virgil's *Bucolics* (III, 65) and is the second part of a verse composed by the shepherd Demetus in honour of the fair Galatea with whom he is in love. The first line, *Malo me Galatea petit, lasciva puella*, ('Galatea, the Wanton maiden, throws an apple at me'), can just be made out in the fragments of a half-erased inscription which appear on the arch of the bridge: *Malo... Ga... Lasciva... puella.*

The picture dates from about 1780. The date is established by its resemblance to the *Windmill at Charenton* from this period (exhibited at the Exhibition of Hubert Robert's Work in Paris, 1933, No 76).

It was in the D. Shchukin Collection, Moscow; then in the State Pushkin Museum of Fine Arts, Moscow; transferred to the Hermitage in 1933.

Literature:
Cat. 1958, I, p. 336, No 7732; T. D. Kamenskaya, *Hubert Robert*, Leningrad, 1939, pp. 22, 23, plate 10; I. S. Nemilova, 'Kartiny Hubert "a Robert" a na literaturnye syuzhety', *Trudy Gosudarstvennogo Ermitazha*, I, 1956, pp. 207–214.

85 ADAM ELSHEIMER
(1578–1610)

ST CHRISTOPHER
oil on copper, 22.5 × 17.5 cm

The work was painted *c.* 1600, during the artist's stay in Venice, when he was influenced by Tintoretto and Bassano.

In the early nineteenth century the George Walker Collection, England, had another picture of the same subject; an engraving of it was made by J. Heath in 1812 (Nagler, 6). To judge by the engraving, the canvas was identical with the Hermitage version. The present whereabouts of the picture from the Walker Collection are unknown; so that it is impossible to establish with certainty the relationship of the two pictures. The opinion of Waizsäker, that the Hermitage version (known to him only from reproductions) is a copy, is not convincing in view of the outstanding quality of the painting. All the other specialists agree that the Hermitage version is authentic.

Elsheimer made considerable advances in the rendering of light by pictorial means, and his influence on the formation of chiaroscuro techniques in West European seventeenth-century painting is as important as that of his contemporary Caravaggio. In the *St Christopher* the artist deliberately avoided the use of perspective common in all Renaissance painting in the landscape background, and created the illusion of space by the simple device of juxtaposing the moonlit figure and the light of the distant lantern. This device was imitated by Elsheimer's pupils, and later, in the 1630s, was an important influence on the evolution of the art of Rembrandt.

Acquired for the Hermitage before 1797.

Literature:
Cat. 1916, No 1984; Cat. 1958, II, p. 337, No 694; Willi Drost, *Adam Elsheimer und sein Kreis*, Potsdam, 1933, pp. 44, 45; H. Weizsäker, *Adam Elsheimer, der Maler von Frankfurt*, I, Berlin, 1936, p. 327; A. N. Izergina and A. N. Nemilov, *Iskusstvo Germanii i Avstrii XV–XIX vv. Gosudarstvenny Ermitazh, putevoditel po vystavke*, Moscow, 1955, p. 23.

CHRISTOPHER PAUDISS
(1618–1666)

STILL-LIFE
oil on canvas (transferred from panel), 62 × 46.5 cm

Signed and dated at bottom, on the edge of the table: *Christopher Paudiss 1660* (the date shows that the picture was painted in Dresden).

This is one of the few still-lives by Paudiss and it reveals his considerable ability and his originality better than any other of his works. Paudiss's style was formed during the period of his work in the studio of Rembrandt, and is greatly influenced by the Dutch school. The softness of the brushwork which can be seen in the Hermitage picture anticipates Chardin's manner; and each individual object has a life of its own, although it is in no way idealized. In this, Paudiss is following the earlier tradition of German still-life painting established by Ludger Tom-Ring and Georg Flegel.
The soft silvery light in which Paudiss's picture is bathed is one of its main charms; the artist could only have learnt how to achieve this effect from Rembrandt.

Acquired for the Hermitage in 1853.

Literature:
Cat. 1916, No 1356; Cat. 1958, II, p. 326, No 1035; A. N. Izergina and A. N. Nemilov, *Iskusstvo Germanii i Avstrii. Gosudarstvenny Ermitazh, putevoditel po vystavke*, Moscow, 1955, p. 24; A. N. Izergina, *Nemetskaya zhivopis XVII v.*, Leningrad, 1960, p. 48.

87 DANIEL SCHULTZ
(1615–1683)

PORTRAIT OF A MONGOLIAN MERCHANT
WITH HIS FAMILY
oil on canvas, 166×231 cm

Signed (the signature is partly illegible) and dated
at the right: *D. Schultz anᵒ. 1664.*

Painted during the artist's residence at Gdansk,
this is the most important picture by the master,
who worked mainly for the Warsaw and Stockholm
aristocracy and for the great merchants of Gdansk.
The sitter, who is not mentioned in any surviving
document, may have been one of the foreign merchants who visited Gdansk, which was then an
international port.
The picture is in the tradition of Dutch family portraiture, and is very close to the work of Bartolom-
mäus van der Helst; it is an outstanding achievement. The technique shows great originality:
Schultz made considerable use of resin-like pigments based on asphaltum, because of which the
canvas is now in a poor state of preservation.

The work was in the palace of Catherine II in the
Tsarskoye Selo in the mid-eighteenth century, and
was transferred to the Hermitage in 1937.

Literature:
Cat. 1958, II, p. 333, No 8540. A. N. Benois,
*Tsarskoye Selo v tsarstvovaniye imperatritsy Elizavety
Petrovny*, St Petersburg, 1910, pp. 132, 134; A. N.
Izergina and A. N. Nemilov, *Iskusstvo Germanii
i Avstrii. Gosudarstvenny Ermitazh, putevoditel po vystavke*, Moscow, 1955, p. 24; A. N. Izergina, *Nemetskaya zhivopis XVII v.*, Leningrad, 1960, pp. 51–
55, pl. 18–21.

BALTHASAR DENNER
(1685–1749)

PORTRAIT OF AN OLD WOMAN
oil on copper, 37×31.5 cm

Balthasar Denner, a resident of Hamburg, was one of the leading portrait painters in the north of Germany. He worked both for townsfolk, and for the nobility. Many of his portraits are distinguished by the softness of the modelling, and the delicacy of his touch. But it was with his portraits of old people that Denner made a name for himself. He specialized in producing small portraits of old men and women. In this he followed the tradition of the later period of the Dutch school, when technical brilliance had supplanted the realistic approach of its greatest period. The *Portrait of an Old Woman* is typical of Denner's work in this vein. The artist does not try to reveal the subject's personality or to give an idea of her inner life, but he aims at achieving the greatest possible precision in rendering the purely outward appearance of the face of an aged person. The network of lines on the faded skin of the old woman, and every crease and pore, are painted with minute thoroughness.
Because of this Denner was nicknamed 'Poren-Denner'. His superficial but skilful paintings, of which he generally made several replicas, enjoyed immense popularity in the eighteenth century.

Acquired for the Hermitage before 1797. There is a version of the picture, with the same model, in a private collection in New York.

Literature:
Cat. 1916, No 1285; Cat. 1958, II, p. 310, No 1326.

89 ANTON RAPHAEL MENGS
(1728–1779)

SELF-PORTRAIT
oil on panel, 104×77 cm

The name of Mengs, the friend of Winckelmann, is associated in the history of German art with classicism. But the master did not avoid a certain eclecticism in his work; nor was he altogether free from the influence of the Academic School of Italian seventeenth-century painting. This, however, did not prevent him from gaining a reputation as an innovator, or from enjoying immense success with the contemporary public. Mengs's portraits are the most valuable part of his artistic heritage. Here Mengs rejected the conventions of classicism, and fused the high artistic ideals of eighteenth-century portrait painting with that new conception of human personality which was just then emerging in German art.

Mengs produced his self-portrait not just to record his features but to glorify the high mission of an artist by investing his personality with an heroic and monumental character. Although the master chose to paint himself wearing his dressing-gown, with his hair slightly dishevelled, he is exceptionally dignified. The pose and the gesture are lofty and grand. The scale of the picture adds to the general impression. The fine heavy features of the artist's face are full of purpose and energy. The palette in his hand is the noble symbol which expresses his sublime mission.

There are several replicas, and a number of versions of the portrait, of which the most important is in the Pitti Palace, Florence.

Acquired for the Hermitage between 1774 and 1783.

Literature:
Cat. 1916, No 1303; Cat. 1958, II, p. 324, No 113; Richard Muther, *Istoriya zhivopisi v XIX v.*, Saint Petersburg, 1899, vol. I, p. 67; H. Schmitz, *Kunst und Kultur des XVIII Jahrhundert in Deutschland*, 1922, p. 258, pl. 138.

90 FRANZ ANTON MAULPERTSCH
    (1724–1796)

THE BAPTISM OF THE EUNUCH
oil on canvas, 50.5×34.5 cm

This small sketch, painted *c.* 1750, shows us the pictorial genius of Maulpertsch as clearly as any of his decorative compositions; Maulpertsch was one of the outstanding masters of the German eighteenth-century Baroque. The subject is taken from the New Testament (Acts VIII, 26–39).
The broad, free strokes and the forms suggested by a few touches of the brush give the picture its expressive and emotional appeal. The dynamic composition with the scene of the baptism placed in the bottom left corner, the landscape, which is barely indicated, with no horizon, a cloudy sky and the silhouette of a tree bent by the wind, all combine to create the impression of a scene which is set in the infinite, beyond the limits of reality. This does not seem to be an independent composition, but is probably the sketch for a larger monumental painting.
In the National Museum in Warsaw is a picture which was painted after this sketch; it used to be described as the work of an unknown artist, until it was recently attributed to Johann Georg Trautmann by Bruno Buschart. An etching of the picture was made by J. A. Nothnagel.

Transferred to the Hermitage in 1925 from the Yusupov Collection as the work of an unknown Italian artist.

Literature:
Cat. 1958, II p. 366, No 5758; M. Shcherbacheva, 'Eskiz Maulpertscha v Ermitazhe', *Soobshcheniya Gosudarstvennogo Ermitazha*, 1956, X, p. 36; Klara Garas, *Franz Anton Maulpertsch*, Budapest, 1960, Cat. No 20; Bialostocki, *Europäische Malerei*, 1957, p. 547, fig. 396; *The Burlington Magazine*, 1957, XCIX; Bruno Buschart, 'Johann Georg Trautmann der Meister der Frankfurter Salome', *Pantheon*, 1963 (May-June).

91

JOSHUA REYNOLDS
(1723–1792)

CUPID UNTYING THE GIRDLE OF VENUS
oil on canvas, 127.5 × 101 cm

Painted between 1784 and 1788 but not quite finished, this picture stands out from the comparatively few mythological subjects painted by Reynolds because of its rich 'Venetian' colouring, inspired by Titian. The dark red of the drapery, arranged like a tent, which serves as a background for the figure of Venus, the blue-green of the distant landscape on the left of the canvas, and the prevailing golden tonality, reveal the extent of Reynolds's debt to the great sixteenth-century Italian colourist. But at the same time the work is typically English; the design, and particularly the gesture of Venus covering her face with the back of her hand, are typical of the psychological approach of eighteenth-century painting which is so far removed from the clarity of Renaissance art.
The little Cupid is not like any Italian putto; he is the type of playful and mischievous boy which Reynolds loved to paint in his famous portraits of children.
Cupid untying the Girdle of Venus does not illustrate any definite episode from a myth; it is an intimate family scene, showing a young mother playing with her healthy, joyful child. The wings on the boy's back are no more than ornaments to emphasize the softness and flexibility of the body of a young child.
The Hermitage picture is one of the versions of a composition which Reynolds repeated in the course of his career. The earliest version, *The Snake in the Grass*, painted in 1784, is now at the National Gallery, London; others are in the Sloane Museum, and in some private collections in England.

The face of Venus is a portrait; but the identification of the sitter is very difficult, since we can only see a part of her face. One of many controversial opinions as to the identity of Reynolds's model deserves special attention; it is the view of the author of the catalogue of the 1906 Exhibition of Eighteenth-century Art in Paris, that Venus is possibly a portrait of Emma, Lady Hamilton (c. 1761–1815). Lady Hamilton (born Emma Lyon) was a celebrated beauty of her day, who had begun life as a maid and then became a painter's model; she was later married to Sir William Hamilton, British Ambassador at Naples, whom she left for Lord Nelson.

Acquired for the Hermitage in 1791 with the collection of Prince G. A. Potemkin who bought it in 1788 from the artist himself through the agency of Lord Carysfort for £ 105.

Literature:
Cat. 1902 and 1916, No 1390; Cat. 1958, II, p. 385, No 1320; *Sir Joshua Reynolds's Notes and Observations on Pictures… with an Appendix, containing a Transcript of Sir Joshua's Account-Book*, edited by William Cotton, December 1858, p. 86; Ch. Leslie and Tom Taylor, *The Life and Times of Sir Joshua Reynolds*, II, London, 1865, footnote p. 538; A. Graves and W. V. Cronin, *A History of the Works of Sir Joshua Reynolds*, London, 1899–1901, pp. 1210–1213; *Catalogue de l'exposition d'œuvres d'art du XVIIIe siècle à la Bibliothèque Nationale*, Paris, 1906, p. 152; E. K. Waterhouse, *Reynolds*, London, 1941, p. 75; A. E. Kroll, *Angliiskaya Zhivopis XVI–XIX vv. v Ermitazhe*, Leningrad, 1961, pp. 11, 80, 85; E. G. Lissenkov, *Angliiskoye iskusstvo XVIII v.*, Leningrad, 1964, p. 149.

92

THOMAS GAINSBOROUGH
(1727–1788)

PORTRAIT OF THE DUCHESS OF BEAUFORT (?)
oil on canvas, 76.5×63 cm

Painted in the 1770s, this is one of the best portraits by Gainsborough. In it his free and brilliant technique with its exceptional boldness and energy creates a vision of poetic beauty and female grace. The thinnest possible layer of paint—so thin indeed that the weave of the canvas shows through—shapes the gentle face and the faint blush on her cheek, the pensive brown eyes under the dark eyebrows and the half-parted lips. The powdered hair in its complex coiffure frames the face with a greyish-blue halo; for the strands of hair at the temples Gainsborough used vigorous brush-strokes like pencil lines. The diaphanous white fabric of the dress, which changes to a greyish hue in the shadows, clings softly to the sloping shoulders. The portrait seems to be saturated with pale blue, although the only objects of this colour are the silk scarf which the lady holds by the tips of her aristocratic fingers, and the ribbon on the coquettish hat adorned with ostrich feathers.

The identity of the model has not been established beyond doubt. In the catalogue of Gainsborough's paintings attached to the monograph *Thomas Gainsborough* by W. Armstrong (1899) the picture is listed as *Portrait of a Lady in Blue*. E. Waterhouse, in his monograph on Gainsborough (1958), placed the portrait in his list of unidentified sitters. G. Bazin, in his publication *Les grands maîtres de la peinture à l'Ermitage*, follows Waterhouse and calls the Hermitage picture *Portrait d'une dame en bleu*. The name of the Duchess of Beaufort was first mentioned in connection with our picture by P. P. Weiner, in an article on the collection of A. Z.

Khitrovo in the magazine *Starye Gody* (1912) which names A. Z. Khitrovo as the author of this conjecture. The only Duchess of Beaufort who could have sat for this portrait was Lady Elizabeth (d. 1823), daughter of Admiral Boscowen, and wife of Henry, fifth Duke of Beaufort. It is not possible to tell whether she was the sitter for this picture, as the only well-authenticated portrait of this duchess painted by Reynolds was destroyed in a fire in Belvoir Castle in 1816. A certain resemblance has been noticed between the woman in the Hermitage picture, and a Mrs Elliott-Dalrymple, who was twice painted by Gainsborough. But so far it has not been proved conclusively that these two women are one and the same person. The date of the work has not been established with sufficient accuracy. Weiner places the portrait among the 'blue pictures' painted by Gainsborough as a reaction to Reynolds's attack on the blue tones at the end of 1778. But technically the Hermitage portrait differs from Gainsborough's work of the late 1770s, although the coiffure of the model is in the fashion of 1778.

The picture was bequeathed to the Hermitage in 1916 by A. Z. Khitrovo, a Petrograd art-collector. The owner may have purchased it from Ch. Wertheimer, a London antiquary, before 1892.

Literature:
Cat. 1958, II, p. 375, No 3509; W. Armstrong, *Thomas Gainsborough*, Paris, 1899, p. 198; P. P. Weiner, 'Sobraniye A. Z. Khitrovo', *Starye Gody*, 1912, III, p. 3; A. E. Kroll, 'Vystavka portreta', *Iskusstvo*, 1938, No 4, p. 42; A. Kroll, *Angliiskiye portrety*, Leningrad, 1939, pp. 21, 22, 45; Ellis Waterhouse, *Gainsborough*, London, 1958, No 792; G. Bazin, *Les grands maîtres de la peinture à l'Ermitage*, Paris, 1958, pp. 194, 250, pl. 201; A. Kroll, *Gainsborough. Portret gertsogini de Beaufort*, Leningrad, 1960; A. E. Kroll, *Angliiskaya zhivopis XVI–XIX vv. v Ermitazhe*, Leningrad, 1961, pp. 17, 81, 85.

93 JOSEPH WRIGHT OF DERBY
(1734–1797)

THE FORGE
oil on canvas, 105 × 140 cm

Signed and dated at bottom right, on the hammer
lying on the floor: *J. Wright pinxit 1773*

The Hermitage picture is one of a series of works
of this subject, which were produced by Wright
in the early 1770s. Several versions are known in
English private collections: one is in the collection
of the British Association for the Advancement of
Science, dated 1771 (from the collection of Lord
Melbourne), another, dated 1771, is in the collection of Mr Greg (from the Alexander Collection),
and another, dated 1772, was in the collection of
the late Countess Mountbatten of Burma (from the
collection of Lord Palmerston). The Hermitage
painting, with its emphatic contrast between the
cool colours of the night landscape and the fiery
glow of the molten metal, is a beautiful example of
the somewhat theatrical and rationalistic roman-
ticism with which Wright introduced industrial
themes into English art.

The original use of the light effects in *The Forge* is
typical of Wright: the strangely shaped, thick
shadows do not distort the faces and silhouettes of
the figures but emphasize their forms and contours.
To help him paint his artificially lighted pictures,
Wright had a special screen, which was constructed
like a polyptych, and which reached from floor to
ceiling of his studio. The wings were placed at an
angle to each other, and partitioned off part of the
room. Each wing consisted of a number of hinged
and movable wooden frames with black paper
stretched over them. The object to be painted was
placed behind the screen in a stream of light, so
that it appeared to be on a stage.

In his account-book Wright noted down an idea
for a picture of a blacksmith's shop: 'Two men
forming a bar of iron into a horse shoe, from
whence the light must proceed. An idle fellow
may stand by the anvil in a time-killing posture,
his hands in his bosom, or yawning with his arms
stredched upwards, a little twisting of the body.
Horse shoes hanging upon ye walls, and other
necessary things faintly seen, being remote from
the light.' This idea has been partly realized in
the Hermitage picture, partly in the other versions
of the subject.

Exhibited for the first time in the Exhibition of the
Society of Artists of Great Britain in 1773.

Purchased from the artist in 1774 by Catherine II,
for £136, 10s.

Literature:
Cat. 1958, II, p. 383, No 1349. W. Bemrose, *The
Life and Works of Joseph Wright, A.R.A.*, with a
Preface by Cosmo Monkhouse, London, 1885, pp.
13, 30, 35; A. Benois, 'Joseph Wright, Kuznitsa',
V. sb. Gosudarstvenny Ermitazh, I, Petrograd, 1921,
pp. 37–42; A. Kroll, *Joseph Wright, Kuznitsa*, Lenin-
grad, 1948; B. Nicolson, 'Joseph Wright's Early
Subject Pictures', *The Burlington Magazine*, 1954
(March), pp. 72–80; *Joseph Wright of Derby. An
Exhibition of Paintings and Drawings*, Catalogue by
Benedict Nicolson, The Arts Council of Great Brit-
ain, 1958; A. E. Kroll, *Angliiskaya zhivopis XVI–
XIXvv. v Ermitazhe*, Leningrad, 1961, pp. 15, 81, 86.

94 JOHN HOPPNER
(1759–1810)

PORTRAIT OF R. B. SHERIDAN (?)
oil on canvas, 77×64 cm

The portrait was painted *c.* 1790. The traditional identification of the sitter as Richard Brinsley Sheridan (1751–1816), the English dramatist and parliamentarian, seems doubtful. The figure in the well-known portrait of Sheridan painted by Hoppner, which was bought in 1921 by E. E. Leggatt (from the Harland-Peck Collection), is not the same as the model in the Hermitage picture. Sheridan was painted by other famous English portrait painters, including Gainsborough, Reynolds and the pastel painter and draughtsman John Russell; but none of the known portraits of Sheridan by these artists is at all close to the sitter in the Hermitage canvas. The portrait which was engraved in 1791 by J. F. Bolt (executed in stipple), in which Sheridan was painted against the background of the Palace of Westminster, is closer to the Hermitage painting than any of the others.
Hoppner, a gifted but rather superficial portraitist who enjoyed tremendous popularity among the aristocracy, was influenced by stronger artistic personalities. The influence of Reynolds was the most important factor in the formation of his style.

Hoppner's late works are influenced by Romney and, to an even greater extent, by Lawrence. The noble and reserved *Portrait of Sheridan* is in the style of Reynolds. The colour scheme of the portrait which is based on a refined combination of greyish-brown, green and pale blue colours laid on in flowing free strokes, admirably displays the brilliance of Hoppner's technique when he was at the height of his powers.

Bequeathed to the Hermitage in 1916 by A. Z. Khitrovo, Petrograd.

Literature:
Cat. 1958, II, p. 390, No 3510; Julia Franken, 'Mr Harland-Peck's Collection', *The Connoisseur*, 1903, V, VI, p. 84; P. P. Weiner, 'Sobraniye A. Z. Khitrovo', *Starye Gody*, 1912, III, p. 3; *The Year's Art*, 1921, p. 290; A. E. Kroll, *Angliiskaya zhivopis XVI–XIX vv. v Ermitazhe*, Leningrad, 1961, pp. 13, 81, 85; E. G. Lissenkov, *Angliiskoye iskusstvo XVIII v.*, Leningrad, 1964, p. 168.

95 GEORGE MORLAND
(1763–1804)

APPROACHING STORM
oil on canvas, 85 × 117 cm

Signed and dated on the tree-trunk at the bottom
right: *G. Morland 1791*

The Hermitage painting is one of the few large
pictures by Morland which are highly finished;
most of his works were done in a hurry and never
completed.
Morland painted storm subjects several times. It
does not seem possible to identify the Hermitage
landscape with any of the master's works which
are mentioned in exhibitons, or listed in the mono-
graphs devoted to his *œuvre*.
The *Stormy Landscape with a Rider* which appeared
in the Bukowski sale of 1935 (Stockholm) is very
close to the Hermitage version. It is almost identical with the *Approaching Storm* in composition, and
is nearly the same in size (83×116 cm).
The *Approaching Storm* reveals the main features of
Morland's art in the early 1790s: the keen feeling
for nature, the great skill in arranging the individual elements of the landscape which he combined
with the clever choice of detail and the rejection
of all that is superfluous. The drama of the sky is
sensitively related to the earth where a lull seems
to reign before the storm breaks. The turbulent
romantic mood which pervades the scene gives
a dynamic quality to this quiet countryside. The
surface of the canvas has been given the same
dynamic quality: the contours and outlines of the
objects are painted with vigorous and sure strokes
but the rest of the picture—especially the foliage—
is painted in narrow undulating strokes which
form a rhythmical pattern.

Acquired by the Hermitage in 1919, formerly in the
collection of Count Fersen, Petrograd; it had
been in this collection as early as 1850.

Literature:
Cat. 1958, II, p. 381, No 5834; *Ukazatel sobraniyu
kartin i redkikh proizvedenii khudozhestva, prinadlezha-
shchikh chlenam imperatorskogo doma i chastnym litsam
Peterburga*, Saint Petersburg, 1861, p. 32; G. C.
Wiliamson, *George Morland*, London, 1907; H. Bukowski, *Konst auktion 21/22-II-1935*, Stockholm, No
299; A. E. Kroll, *G. Morland. Approaching Storm*.
Leningrad, 1948, A. E. Kroll, *Angliiskaya zhivopis
XVI–XIX vv. v Ermitazhe*, Leningrad, 1961, pp. 16,
82, 86; A. E. Kroll, *Morland i yego kartiny v Ermitazhe*, Leningrad, 1963; E. G. Lissenkov, *Angliiskoye
iskusstvo XVIII v.*, Leningrad, 1964, p. 201.